Cashville Let's Get This Money

Kevin (K-Rob) Robinson

© 2022 Kevin Robinson

All rights reserved. No part of this book may be reproduced or transmitted in any form or by means, electronic or mechanical, including photocopying, recording, or by any information storage and retrieval system, without written permission from publisher.

Published in Nashville, Tennessee, *by BN Publication LLC*

While some incidents in this book are true, the names and personal characteristics of those described have been changed in order to protect their privacy. Any resemblance to persons living or dead is entirely incidental and unintentional.\

Copyright 2022

ISBN- 9798840897973

Cover art and illustration by Rafiqshah

Author: Kevin Robinson

PRINTED IN THE UNITED STATES OF AMERICA

Dedication

This book is dedicated to all the young boys who is still looking for their purpose in life. I pray this book helps you on your journey to becoming a man.

-KROB

Chapter 1

Growin' up in the hood, I was exposed to the daily hand to hand tussle of street life that young suburban kids dream about. If you're from the hood, then you know what I mean 'cause you see, your hood and my hood are the same. The same stuff that goes on in your hood, goes on in mine too.

My hood is in Nashville, Tennessee; but don't let Nashville musical heritage and country popularity fool you. We're pressing up more than just records and hits ain't just in the box office, Nashville endures a healthy and virile street life. I should know. This mysterious riddle, I call my life, began there.

My house, well, my grandmother's house was just a few blocks from where all the action took place. From my vantage point, I could hear the reports of gunshots mingled with the street life and ghetto mayhem.

Young thugs would pass back and forth in front of my grandmother's house, as they would pass my eyes would shine at them; but my grandmother would talk to me daily about not growing up to be like the boys on the corner. I can still hear her telling me to "Stay in school and get a good job." I would always listen and try to understand what she was saying, knowing that she only wanted what was best for me.

My best friend was a kid named Danny. He was like a brother to me and if you saw Danny you were bound to see me also. Danny lived around the corner from me with his mother, in one of the most drug infested projects in the city. One bad thing was his mother had gotten caught up in a life of drug abuse and reluctantly, she had to let

Danny's little brother and sister go live with other relatives. Danny really resented the situation and would never talk about it. He refused to leave. He felt an obligation to stay and help take care of his mother. When we were young, Danny and I would always find a way to make some extra money. We first started out selling candy for our elementary school. We would go to the other side of town and charge 50 cents extra to every bag of candy we sold.

A few years later when we were much older, my grandmother suggested that we start mowing the lawn for her church, as a way for us to earn some money. We had no idea that it would blossom into a full-fledged business. Danny and I would take great pride in the work we were doing. We would cut fancy designs in the lawn and make creatively designed flower beds around the church. When members of the congregation saw our work, they began to ask us to come to their homes and do work for them. This enterprise enabled us to have a few dollars in our pockets and I always saved my money, but Danny start experimenting with weed (marijuana) and began to spend a lot of his money on it.

One day I thought about all the money Danny and the other people in the neighborhood was spending on weed, I decided I would invest my money and make a profit by selling weed. Even if all else failed, Danny would be my best customer and I would still get more out of it than I put in.

I presented the idea to Danny and he thought it was a great plan. He said that he would make sure I got the best weed he could find. Danny showed me how to bag it up into 5 and 10 dollar bags, known as "nickels" and "dimes" in the hood. He said that we would sell more that way because no one sold nickels anymore, but that everyone could afford a dime bag.

Danny started telling everyone we knew that he had the best weed, plus he had the nickel bags and things started moving from there. I didn't think it would be like this.

Danny and I came up with a system, because he was so popular in the hood where all the action was, he would do all the selling and I would handle of the finances, storage and bagging.

School was about to start back and business would be even better, but every day I would tell Danny that he should stop smoking. Not that he started acting crazy when he smoked, I just thought that we should sell it all.

When school started back, Danny and I tried to get the same schedule, but it did not work. I even tried to persuade the teacher to put us together so I could help him with his studies, but that was denied too. I knew without me, Danny's survival in school was greatly limited.

    At school, we ran into some old friends, Mark and Dante. Mark was very popular in school and lived on the other side of town. He was very friendly and did not get into trouble, but he had some hustle in him and I liked that. Dante was a wild one and did not take nothing off of anyone, but he and Mark were a duo, just like Danny and I. They both were down for making some money, so we put them on. We would pay them a dollar for every nickel bag they sold and $2 for every dime bag they sold. If they could sell forty to fifty bags a day, that would be some decent money, and they could.

Later on, it came to my attention that they were selling joints at $3.00 a pop and they were getting about five joints out of one nickel bag. They were clearing a profit of about $11.00 a bag on every nickel they could sell like this; and from what I heard, they were selling a lot. I knew they were hustlers from the beginning, so I wasn't mad. Danny on the other hand, didn't see it that way.

I tried to convince Danny for us to team up with Dante and Mark, because I already could see how we could take over Nashville together. So I went and spoke with Mark and Dante to see how they felt about this idea.

    "Sounds good, but how?" Dante asked.

    "Let's become partners." I said.

    "Are you serious?" asked Mark.

It took me a minute to convince Danny to go for the joint venture idea, but I told him that these guys were team players and that with them on our side we had the makings for some serious money-making potential.

    "Just trust me, please!" I said. And he did.

So this was the lay-out. Danny would continue to insure that we had the best weed on the block and he would control his hood. Mark and Dante would take over the school and their sides of town and I would handle the finances. As we talked, it was evident that things for all of us were about to change in a very drastic way.

To start things off, we agreed to invest in a pound of weed with everyone investing $250 a piece; and that was the day that Danny stopped smoking.

Danny got the weed and we met up at his house in the projects. I put the word down to Mark and Dante not to say anything negative about Danny's situation, because it was a sore spot for him.

When we entered the apartment, there were people sitting all over the place. We just moved quietly through to Danny's room. The first thing that we did was bag up half pound in nickel bags and dime bags, then we started rolling joints that would be a good profit. As soon as we made our first thousand, we intended to buy another pound.

By the end of the week, we copped two more pounds. In the second week, we got four more pounds; and by the fourth week, we had copped seven more pounds!

We had the hood, the school, and all the old heads lock. It was crazy. At the end of six weeks, we were sitting on a little over forty grand!

Chapter 2

Danny had mentioned the idea of selling cocaine, but at the time we didn't know much about it, so we continued to play towards our strength- the weed business. Danny said that he would find out the prices and a little more information on how to go about selling cocaine.

At this particular point in time, we paid ourselves $500 a week. The rest, we put back into the business. With this budget, the money just kept getting bigger and better. By Christmas break, the school was starting to get hot on Mark, so he had to cool out, not that he would.

"Mark, you've got to chill out a lil' bit at the school, because everyone is talking about you," I said. "If you do, I guarantee you that we are going to be getting some serious paper real soon."

Mark, Dante and Danny stayed in the mall shopping. I would not do it, because I couldn't bring in a bunch of new clothes to my grandmother's house like that. My grandmother was already suspicious of me and my friends, because she would see Danny bringing in all types of clothes to the dry cleaners where she worked.

By the end of the school year, Danny, Mark and Dante were hot as hell! I continued to keep a low profile myself. In school, I was an 'A' and 'B' student. I loved school, plus attending school and keeping up my good grades, was my way of showing my grandmother that I loved her and appreciate all that she had done for me.

School was about to be out for the summer, and Danny was talking about buying this car from a guy he knew. One of the main problems was Danny did not have a driver's license. I thought he was crazy, but to Danny, buying a car just because he could, was the most logical move he could make. I attributed his thinking to the culture he was deeply entrenched in, because he had been in the hood all of his natural life.

Just before school let out, my grandmother asked me when we were going to start back cutting the church lawn, not to mention the fact that a lot of our old customers were beginning to ask about us coming back to work their yards. I knew that Danny was not up to it, but I had to take care of it or my grandmother would grow more suspicious of me.

I knew I could not do all the work by myself, so I hired two Mexicans to work with me. Danny would laugh at me when he would drive by, seeing me cutting the yards that we used to cut, knowing we had the weed business on lock-down. He knew I did it for my grandmother and that, at times, made it not so funny. One thing Danny didn't know, I was starting to see this as a business that would benefit us both in the long run. That summer, the lawn business grew even bigger. I had to hire two more people. We had it set up where on Wednesdays, we would get together to bag up more weed and see how everything was going.

By the end of the summer, Danny began to talk more about selling cocaine. I'd see firsthand, the dangers of this new game, but I had also seen its benefits. I had always said that we were quite fortunate up to this point, not to have had any drama. But I was beginning to wonder how long we could avoid it, because if we delved into the cocaine business, something bad was bound to happen.

We were making lots of money. Everything was going good. Danny had fixed his car up and was talking of buying a Cadillac.

One week before school was scheduled to begin, we had a meeting at Danny's house. At the meeting, Danny announced that it was time, that we made a move with cocaine. I was hesitant about handling this new product.

"Alright. I'm in," I said, feeling compelled to acquiesce. "But, we are not gonna be suckered into this game blindly, so let's look at what we're getting into."

Danny spoke up first. "I've already got a couple of boys slanging weed who say that they can move this product like water!" "What about the competition?" asked Dante.

"Danny has been in his hood since the beginning of time, whose gonna question his credibility to get paper from his own backyard?" Mark stated.

Mark had a good point, I had to admit. So, we were off. Danny had paid a junkie to teach him how to cook, because we refused to allow anyone outside of our clique, to have access to what we were doing. I knew that we should keep this among ourselves.

Once it was cooked, Danny chopped it up and bagged it up. Danny began to distribute samples; in fact, we decided to give away 2 of our 4 and half ounces free. Mark and Dante would continue selling the weed until we figure out what our next move would be.

All I had to do was keep the money straight, but by this time, that had already become a job. It was about time to end the lawn business for the season. School was going to start back and this was one break that I was looking forward to.

It took Danny two months to get himself situated where everything was flowing smoothly; but once he established himself as a factor in the hood and on the block, he went from pushing 4 and a half ounces a week to double that! The money was rolling into our pockets like we had never seen.

In two months, Danny had become more than just a player in the game. So when school finally started back, Danny decided that he was not going to go. I did not like that at all, but when Dante and Mark followed his lead, I had no choice but to accept their desires and be the best friend I could be.

"Yo Danny, you're neglecting part of your responsibilities," I said.

"What you mean? I'm moving plenty product."

"That's not what I mean," I said. "What about school?"

"Nah, that's your job. My job is the streets."

I let it go. I loved Danny like a brother, and if this was what he was going to do, then I would go to school for both of us. I stayed in school and was determined to make it.

My grandmother found out what Danny was doing and she brought it to my attention, but I played it off and acted like I did not know about it. I probably could have gotten an Oscar for the Worst Actor Award. She knew he was my best friend and she knew that I would defend him, which I did.

Danny's mother decided to leave drugs alone. I never heard what really happened, but one day she just disappeared, then returned 30 days later, cured of her addiction. She said that she felt as though, she could not continue on the path that she was on, plus she knew it meant a lot to Danny, which was also true. But I would've thought that the fact that one of her closest girlfriends died from an overdose would have factored into the equation, but if it did, she never mentioned it. Her and that lady did everything together. It was so strange, but it made Danny happy and that was what was important to me.

Now, if I thought what we were doing was big, it was only the beginning and I was mistaken.

Chapter 3

This year was a very monumental year for me. For one thing, this was the last year of high school, which definitely changed my life. The second thing was Ashlee.

About one month after school started back, this new girl moved to Nashville from Miami named Ashlee Boycess, a beautiful girl with a wonderful blending of fire and softness. Her beauty was tragic, in that all the guys would sweat her, so she never had a moment's peace. This made her interesting, to say the least.

The first time I saw her, she was walking from the student parking lot, gliding like a beauteous spirit with an unusually effortless grace and free pleasing rhythm. The sweeping of her thighs accentuated a supple waist, which emphasized the lush curve of her breasts. The unique and faultless beauty of flawless body was crowned by a fine-featured face as sweet as dawn. This was a young woman in full bloom. I had paused to watch her undulating hips recede from my vision before I realized that I had a class to get to. That day I was late.

By this time, Danny had finally gotten his license and he bought himself a Cadillac Seville STS with 20 inch rims. It was black, with chrome rims. Mark bought him a Chevy Super sport, and Dante had a Ford Expedition. They were doing big things.

Danny was up early every morning to take me to school. Sometimes if Danny could not make it, he would send Dante or Mark. When school let out, I knew Danny would be right outside on time, 2:30 p.m. every day.

All this time, no one suspected me having anything to do with Mark, Dante or Danny's illegal activities. The usual sign of flashy jewelry, cars and of course dropping out of high school, were not part of my resume. Everyone just assumed that they were my boys, because we were tight when they were in school; plus, I seemed too laid back for hustling. I worked hard to keep a clean image, because I had a goal.

My only luxury was clothing. I always liked to look clean and smell fresh. When I was clean, I felt good about myself and my confidence level stayed high. My desire for clothes was not about labels, it was about how I felt about myself.

I decided later, not to close down the lawn business for the season. Instead, I chose to venture into other aspects of the lawn care service, due to the fact that lawn service was important to a lot of people year-round. I hired Mr. James to run the business for me while I was in school. He was a good friend of the family, who had fallen on hard times and needed some help. Occasionally, I still pitched in and helped out though.

Mr. Johnson, down at the neighborhood store, was talking to Danny about selling his store. So we decided to swing by there and see if we could work something out.

"Whatever he wants for the store, between the four of us, we can handle it easily," Danny said.

"If we're gonna get it, let's get it the right way," I said. "I set up the bank accounts for just this reason. Did y'all get your vehicles in the way that I asked you to?"

When everyone decided to get cars, I recommended that they used their bank accounts and their fictitious jobs as a reference. I realized that we would need credit, and this was my way of paving the way for the future. A month after they got their cars, they received credit cards in the mail. They did not realize the significance of them, but now they would be able to see that, not only were we street credible, but also recognized as legit.

The store was nice. It had two main employees beside Mr. Johnson. Mr. Ed worked the meat counter and Mrs. Parker worked the cash register.

Mr. Johnson had plenty of money and had lost his interest in dealing with the day to day operations concerned with running the store. Mr. Johnson was also the local numbers man, but he said he was not trying to part with that. He said as long as we could get an adult to purchase the store from him, he would sell it to us.

I called our lawyer and accountant, who set us up with the paper work we needed, then we went to a bank and got a loan for the store. We could have bought that store straight out, but it was important that these things wouldn't be able to be taken from us. We needed things for the future.

That night the deal was done. Mr. Johnson explained to me how to run the store and he told me, feel free to call on him anytime.
The first thing that Danny wanted to do was fire Mrs. Parker and Mr. Ed. I had to explain to Danny that we needed them to be there, because they had the experience. I intended to make Mrs. Parker the Manager, because she fully understood how to operate all of the day to day routines, so firing them was out.
So we came to an understanding, that Mrs. Parker would manage during the day and we would work nights and weekends. We also gave them both a raise. This way, we insured that they would be satisfied with the new management.
Danny hired his sister to work on the weekends and a couple of nights per week. She really hadn't been able to be a part of his life in such a long time, so for him, this was his way of making up for old times. He also made sure that she had a nice fat check coming to her every week. In the back of the store, there was a game room. After school, there were a lot of people hanging out there.
Back at school, Ashlee started kicking it with this girl named Jalfanine. She was from the neighborhood and she was cool with all of us. Back in the days, her brother used to call shots, but he got killed in a robbery. We were little kids then, so his death did not really affect her too much. Jafinine was growing up to be a very attractive and street-wise sister.
One Saturday afternoon, Ashlee and Jalfanine showed up at the store. I had heard from a few people that they were known to stop by from time to time and play video games in the back, so naturally I figured this was why they were stopping by.

I had been seeing Ashlee around at different spots every now and then, but I hadn't actually allowed her to see me checking her out.

When they walked in the store, I was teaching Danny's sister how to run the register and close it out at night. Danny's sister was actually a very intelligent girl and kinda cute, but she was off limits to me. After they had been in the back for a few minutes, Jalfanine came up front to the counter where I was.

"Hey B.," she said, calling me by the name she had coined when we were kids.

"What's up, J?" I replied, smiling good-naturedly.

"When you get a chance, I need to holla at you about something, alright?"

"Okay. Just give me a minute."

A few times in the past, I had been tempted to try to get with Jafanine, because she was a chocolate cutie with one of the fattest asses, plus she had pretty feet, but the chemistry just wasn't there for anything positive. It would have strictly been a sexual thing for me and I am sure that Jalfanine would not be able to appreciate that in and of itself. As soon as I was finished with Danny's sister, I immediately went to see what Jalfanine wanted. As I approached Jalfanine, I saw that Ashlee was standing on the side of the game Jalfanine was playing, as if like she was hiding.

"What's up B?" Jalfanine said.

I looked at her quizzically. "What's up, J?"

"B, this is my girl Ashlee. Ashlee, this is my boy Billy," she said, then turned back around to her game and left us to get more acquainted with one another.

"How are you, Ashlee?" I said, trying to find some common ground for conversation.

"I'm fine," she said sweetly. "And You?"

"I'm maintaining," I replied, looking deeply into her eyes, thinking this could not be real.

"So tell me Ashlee, whose idea was this?" I asked, referring to the introduction.

"Partly Jalfanine's, and partly mine. But mostly mine," she said with a seductive smile.

"Are you serious?" I asked her with a look that was playful. But, all this time I was wondering what kind of game this beautiful girl was playing. I instantly decided that whatever she was playing, I'd hang around to see.

"Yes."

"What do I have to offer a young woman of your tastes?"

Without a blink or twitch, she confidently responded, "It's not what you have to offer that I am interested in, but there's something unspoken, an air about you that says to me, 'Take a chance', so here I am, taking a chance."

"Ooohhh! You're good!" I said smiling, and interested because I believed her.

"Would you like to go out with me?" she asked.

I hesitated a few seconds, so as not to seem desperate, then I calmly replied, "Yeah...but, then, you already knew that, didn't you?"

"Why?" she asked, ignoring my question.

Thoughtfully, I said, "Because I don't believe you. I want to, but this is too convenient. So, I will go out with you or take you out only because this game is getting interesting and I would like to see where it goes."

"So I guess this means that you are going out with me tomorrow night?"

"I guess it does," I said.

We continued to make small talk, playing with one another's mind, when she boldly took a step that put her inches from my face and me. Not being one to back down from a challenge, I proceed to match her step with one of my own, when Danny pulled up outside of the store, pumping the bumpin' ass 15's he had just installed in the Cadillac.

"Hustlin' to make a million!" boomed the voice.

"That must be my boy," I said quickly, bringing our little game to a halt.

"Here's my number. Call me tonight."

Just as I was turning to leave, Danny came bopping up.

"What's up Ashlee?" giving me five.

"Ain't too much," she replied politely, staring boldly into my eyes.

"Billy, I need to talk to you," he said, adding, "Playa." I knew that was for Ashlee.

I gave her my number, then Danny and I bounced. Inside of the Caddy, Danny lowered the volume on the system and just looked at me smiling like a damn fool.

"What?" I couldn't stand the damn look on his face.

"Boy, you a smooth mutherfucker!" He was pointing at me and laughing.

"I've been trying for months to get her."

"What the hell you mean, I just did me man?!" he said, imitating me. It was funny.

"She sent Jalfanine at me."

"Boy, when I grow up, I wanna be just like you. Fuck Mike!" Danny said as he gently pulled the Caddy out into the traffic.

Up to this point in the game, we had managed to avoid the violence and brutality of the streets. Our success was based too much upon luck, I thought. I began to think more about this every day, as we amassed more capital. How easy it would be for us to lose what we have? I began to get paranoid, so I put great care into our financial security, because if I didn't, we'd be in hot water and it would be all my fault. Why? They could not hide from what they could not see, but because I could see this, I had to protect us all.

The day after Ashlee and I were introduced, she called me that night and we set a date for the next night. I told her I did not have a car. She said she knew and didn't mind.

So the next night, she came to pick me up. She told me to listen for her special horn. I asked her how it would sound, but she told me to just listen for it.

"You can't miss it," she said softly. And she was right.

When she pulled up, I saw her. She was driving a nice BMW 325 convertible with 20" rims on it. I sat there and waited for her to blow her horn. I was curious to hear what it sounded like. "Biiiilllllyyyy! Biiiilllllyyyy!" It was the car! She could record short messages and play them back over the car horn.

I thought to myself that her parents must have some real money because that horn was playful luxury.

"Please, take my name off that thing," I said, smiling at her. I'm sure that could be heard for blocks!"

"I thought you'd find that amusing," she said. "I changed my mind about our plans. Let's be spontaneous."

"I think I'd like some ice cream," I said, saying the exact opposite of what she expected. I wanted her, but it had to be on my terms.

She took me to Red Lobster. "I thought we were going to get ice cream," I said.

"What could be more spontaneous that coming to Red Lobster for ice cream." I thought right then and there, this girl plays some real head games. Where did she get all these games from?

I ended up ordering food for us to eat. While we were waiting, we made more small talk about what we were going to do when we graduated from school and the general plans we had for our lives. Ashlee said that one day she wants a family, but before then she wants to own an expensive clothing store. She also told me about how she used to model and all the places she has been. To me, her life was very interesting and I truly found myself listening to her and not just lusting. Ashlee had a very sharp mind.

After eating, we rode around for hours talking and just enjoying one another's company.

"Billy, you know I know what to do, right?" she had pulled over to a spot on the side of a hill that afforded us a beautiful view of the city.

"Everybody knows what I do." I was trying to resist the temptation to look in her eyes.

"What? You mean the lil' lawn business and the lil' store thang?" she said, speaking of them like they were a joke, and compared to the money I was getting from drugs she was right.

"Yeah," I said, putting my arm over the back of her seat and running my hands through her silky black hair. "That's what I do." I added.

"Nah, brother, let's try this again," she said, turning to face me and softly touching my lips and whispering. "I know about you, Dante, Mark and Danny," she continued.

"And?" I asked, enjoying this game.

"I know," she kissed me lightly and ever so gently. "That you are respected greatly by them," she kissed me again. "I also know that you boys got Nashville on the lock with weed and you're not doing too bad with the other thing," she kissed me once more quickly, offering me more of her mouth, then swiftly slipping out of my grasp and out of the car and into the night air.

I got out of the car too and she was leaning against the hood watching the stars.

"Is this why we're here, because you think I'm some kind of a big baller?" I could feel my blood begin to boil over with disappointment.

"No. we are here because there is an attraction between us."

"Or either we are here because one of us is curious about things that don't concern them." I was a little hot but in control. I would not let her get me off my square, if I could help it.

I burst out laughing. I saw her eyes flash anger but then she removed it and channeled it or something because it was gone. She slowly approached me and placed my hands around he curvy waist, then she placed her hands on the sides of my face gently and kissed me deeply. She held me like she needed me. I melted into her arms, trying to give her just as much as she was giving, yet allowing her to determine just how far this should go.

"I like you, Billy, probably more that I should," she uttered thoughtfully.

"I don't break hearts. I end 'em." Then I grabbed her to me and kissed her softly.

Later that morning as she was driving me home (nothing happened, it was mutually agreed), she told me that Jalfanine had told her all about us and that she did not care. She said that everyone thought I was a choir boy, but that she knew what was going on from day one. She had respected us and kept it a secret. I respected Jalfanine for that, keeping things under wrap, that was cool; but I wondered if I was that transparent, because if Jalfanine saw it, who else could see it? Ashlee pulled up in front of my grandmother's house and turned off her car and pulled up the handbrake.

"Billy, I want you to meet my cousin."

"Who is he?"

"His name is Marco, and he will be in Atlanta for the hair show next week," she said.

I always wanted to visit Atlanta, so I agreed without hesitation. After we talked a little more, I asked her to drop me off at the store. When I got there, I saw that Danny's mother was there with Danny's sister. She was definitely off drugs. By this time, he had bought her a beautiful house on the other side of town. I was surprised to see her over here, because Danny did not like her coming over this side of town and I told her so. But she told me, "Billy, I had Danny, Danny did not have me." I laughed like hell at that. Danny's mother was a very beautiful woman and much different that she used to be. Just seeing her happy and enjoying life for a change made me feel good about the way things were going.

Chapter 4

I called Danny to pick me up and I told him about the meeting with Ashlee's cousin. He wanted to come along, but I told him I got it. Danny dropped me off at home and said he would pick me up in the morning. I told him Dante was coming to drop off some money, so he would take me to school.

"When are you going to buy a car Billy?" Danny asked.

"Now? Man, my grandmother would have a heart attack!"

One thing about Dante, he would always be on time. Now Mark, that's another thing. As Dante was pulling up, Ashlee was pulling up as well. She told Dante we went to the same school, that she would take me. I grabbed the bag with the money and put it in the house. I then told him I'll holla at him later. When I got in the car with Ashlee, she asked, "Do they get tired of getting up to take you to school?"

"They use to go to school with me every morning. They basically stopped going to school, but that never stopped them from taking me."

"Tell them their boss has a new ride," Ashlee said sarcastically. "Can you even drive?"

I laughed as I showed her my driver's license. Right then she pulled over and told me to drive.

"I'm not used to driving my man around."

When we got to school, we ran into Jalfanine.

"Girl, I thought you were coming to pick me up this morning? Jalfanine asked.

"I'm sorry Jalfanine, I forgot."

"I know what was on your mind." she responded, smiling at me.

As we were parting to attend our respective classes, Ashlee asked me to keep her keys because she was taking me home and Jalfanine was going too.

This was the routine all week long. We planned on leaving for Atlanta on Friday night and returning Sunday evening. However, I told my grandmother that I was going over to Danny's for the weekend. It wasn't the best alibi, but it worked.

Everything went as planned. Ashlee and I got together that evening and at 7:00 we picked up Jalfanine. She had never been to Atlanta before and neither had I. I drove while they talked about all the stores they wanted to go shopping in. Ashlee said that her and her mother used to go to Atlanta and shop all the time, which was why she was so familiar with the area.

By the time we hit Chattanooga, they were both asleep. I was driving and thinking to myself about what this meeting was going to be like with her cousin.

When we finally came to the city of Atlanta, I woke them up. Jalfanine's eyes got big, I could tell she was very excited and happy to be here.

Ashlee told me to get off on the Peachtree exit and she would show me the way from there to the hotel. As we pulled into the Marriott, I was a bit excited myself, but I played it cool. We pulled up to the valet parking area, where we got out of the car and they took our bags. Ashlee left for a minute and when she returned, she had the keys to our rooms. I was not sure about the sleeping arrangements, so I freely assumed that Ashlee and Jalfanine would share a room. But then we went to the rooms, I noticed that my baggage was with hers.

The rooms were nice. They had big screen television in them, a Jacuzzi, a fully stocked bar, a king-sized bed and a kitchen. I couldn't believe it.

Ashlee's cousin was staying at another hotel, so she had to page him and let him know that we were here. He called back immediately and said that he would be down in the lobby at 11:30pm.

When Marco, Ashlee's cousin, showed up, he had two Cubans with him; and they were dressed sharp. Marco looked like he was half Hispanic and half American. The more I thought about it, I could see the same traits in Ashlee too. Marco wore a crisp and tailored Italian suit, with soft leather shoes, and on his wrist was a watch whose name I could not pronounce; and from its looks, I probably could not afford it. His two companions were just as sharp.

The two Cubans held conversations with Marco in Spanish, and I could not understand anything that was being said. I felt kinda odd, but was even more thrown off when Ashlee began speaking in Spanish too! I immediately wished that I had learned it from my workers at the landscaping business.

We had a wonderful time, though. Ashlee showed herself to be a most appropriate and exotic hostess, because Jalfanine and I were lost. That night I chatted with Marco mostly about our personal lives until 2am, but the conversation never once drifted towards the direction of why Ashlee had brought me here. I made up my mind that if he doesn't speak on anything pertaining to drugs, I wouldn't either. I responded properly to his comments and questions, then suddenly it dawned on me that Marco and his Cuban partners probably wanted to check me out, to see what type of dude I was.

Marco was definitely feeling Jalfanine, too. They danced and talked all night too. It was evident that they were going to be seeing more of each other.

It seemed to me that the night was ending, Ashlee said that the night had just begun. She said that Atlanta was nothing like Nashville. "This city never sleeps!" So we rode around a few more interesting spots for about an hour and a half, and she was right. The city had plenty of action at night. It was about 4:00am when we decided to call it a night.

Chapter 5

The next day, Marco called around 10:30am. He said that he wanted to take us shopping and he wanted us to be ready at noon. Something told me that today would be about business. Ashlee met me in the living room, dressed in a Dolce and Gabana, crushed silk, two-piece skirt set, with her own matching Dolce and Gabana no heel slip-ons.

As I watched her sway my way, I said, "Let's go baby," shaking my head at how fine she was.

"What?" she asked, as if she didn't know what I was thinking.

We met Marco downstairs in the lobby. Jalfanine was already there; they were waiting for us. We went to the mall and Marco basically set the pace for us. He gave Jalfanine and Ashlee $1,000 a piece! Marco then gave Ashlee his cell phone and told her that he would call them when we return. We then left the mall and Marco did not waste any time. Everything was strictly business.

"The Cuban guys I was with last night were there to meet you and decided if you were the kind of guy we should do business with," he said, as we pulled off in a Jaguar XJ12. "Everything panned out o.k. They like you very much." Then, straight to the point, "How many kilos can you move in a month?"

As much as I wanted to be able to quote a figure, I couldn't. "I need to think about that one for a minute," I said, trying to run the figures in my head.

"What do you think about a hundred for starters?" he asked.

100! I thought to myself. "What's the price range gonna look like?" I asked, masking the fact that I was seriously shaken, because 100 bricks would put us in a whole other level of the game!

"Let's start at $14,500, but the price gets better," he said.

$14,500 sounded damn good and a hundred at this price was even better. But to be honest, I wasn't completely confident that we could move all of this product. I thought it was worth a shot, so I took it. After talking for an hour or so, Marco looked me dead in the eyes and started talking about keeping it real and having no fuckups. He reassured me that if anything went wrong, I could talk to him and we could work it out.

We rode around for another hour ironing out the fine details and then we headed back to the mall to pick up Ashlee and Jalfanine. We made it back to our rooms later that afternoon after we had stopped at a pleasant restaurant and had a bite.

When we got back to the hotel, Ashlee and I decided we were going to call it a day. Marco and Jafanine had other plans.

The next morning, Marco stopped by our room to let me know that someone would be coming to see me next week. Then he said, "Let's get this money."

A week was cool because it bought me time to get with Danny and figure out how we would handle this. Ashlee drove all the way back to Nashville and not once did she ask me what Marco and I talked about.

Once we were back in Nashville, we dropped Jalfanine off and headed to my grandmother's house. I knew my grandmother would be at church, so I told Ashlee to come in for a minute. We talked for about thirty minutes and I thanked her for all she had done that weekend for me. She said it was only the beginning and then I told her to go home and get some rest, because we had school the next day.

I cleared my mind off Ashlee and onto business. I called Danny.

"Yo Danny, I'm back."

"So how did things go?"

"I'd rather talk to you in person," I said.

About twenty minutes later, he was outside waiting for me. I came out and got in the car with him.

"Just drive around," I said.

I told him all about the weekend with Marco and he could not believe it.

"Yo Danny, he wants to start us out with 100 kilos." "100!" he said incredulously.

"Do you think we can handle it?"

"Yeah, but at what price?"

"$14,500," I said calmly, the shock had already worn off me.

"You bullshittin'!"

"Nah, man, I am dead serious."

"Billy, at $14,500, he could've sent us 300. We'll sell them all!"

"How soon can we move them, because he's giving us a month?"

"That's nothing. It's about to be on!" he said excitedly, adding, "I never thought we would blow like this."

"Let's get this money," I said thinking about how this was going to affect our current operations.

Danny said, "I've got to get started putting everything together, but first we've got to get with Mark and Dante."

I could see Danny was thinking about the moves that we would be making.

"Hey Billy, at $14,500, we can sell bricks at $22,500 and pull $8,000 per brick, right? Now, at 100, we will be looking at around $800,000 baby!"

"And Danny, keep in mind that Marco also said that the price would be getting better."

"Billy, you are going to be needing a cell phone, man."

"I don't want one."

"I'm going to pick one up for you anyway. Just keep the ringer off and your grandmother will never know you have a phone."

On the surface I was smiling, but beneath the surface my mind was moving a million miles a minute. Danny dropped me back off at home and I immediately went in and dropped off in a deep sleep.
This weekend had really exhausted me.

Chapter 6

Danny was copping our dope from this other guy named Mack. Mack was known for selling weight. You could go to Mack and buy from one to twenty kilos. Mack was the man. But in this business, you could be selling to someone one minute and buying from the same guy in the next minute, who you were selling to. Danny respected Mack and knew that Mack respected the game. So Danny went to Mack with a deal. When Danny told him the price, Mack wanted to buy them all! Danny decided wisely to sell him only 25, that way we could get more exposure by selling smaller quantities to other guys; and if push comes to shove and we need the sales, then we could sell the rest to Mack. Mack also gave us the paper up front to insure that he got his first. That was love. He also established a trust with us that later would be repaid.

Danny got with Dante and Mark. Dante had a deal set for 25 more and Mark had a deal for 20. By the end of the week, we had all 100 kilos sold before they were even here.

A few days later, my phone rang. It was Ashlee.

"Hey, baby!"

"What's up Ashlee?"

"Where are you?"

"I'm at the store," I said.

"I'm on my way. I've got something for you," she said and hung up quickly.

I was curious about her urgency. Ashlee pulled in front of the store about twenty-five minutes after our conversation. She was driving a van. Jalfanine was driving her car behind her. Ashlee jumped out of the van, gave me a kiss and handed me the keys and said, "Call me when you're done!" Just like that.

I got in the van and noticed a huge crate in the back of the van and it was full of dope! Immediately, I pulled the van around to the back of the store. I called Danny first.

"Yo!" he answered his phone.

"It's on, nigga," I said, trying to contain the rush of adrenaline that I was feeling. "Call Mark and Dante and let's get this money!" I already got the money," he said.

I have had it for two days."

"Call Dante and Mark and meet me at the store."

Everyone showed up at the about the same time. We walked to the back of the store where the van was parked and we began to unload it. Danny already had the money, so he took 25. Dante had 10 sold and said he would be right back. Mark took 20 and left.

Danny came back and said Mack would need 25 more! Mark came back and took five more. By 11pm, we had the money for Marco. I called Ashlee and told her to come through. It took her about 45 minutes and she came with Jalfanine. She gave me a kiss and got in the van with the money and left.

It was late, so I called Danny and told him to get the rest of the money together and come to see me tomorrow after school. The next day Ashlee came and picked me up for school.

"Marco couldn't believe you did all of that in one night," she said. "He told me to tell you to call him."

I called him on his cell phone. "Marco, what's up? Is everything straight?"

"Straight? Hell Yeah! I didn't know you had it like that! I thought it would take you about 2 weeks to handle that," he said.

I told him how things went and the way we had things already set up.

"Ashlee and Jalfanine are coming to Miami next week. Why don't you come down with them?" he asked me.

"Let me think about it," I replied.

When school let out for the day, Dante, Danny and Mark were parked by Ashlee's car. I knew that they were there to pick me up, so I told her that I would call her later. They were riding in Dante's truck. "Turn the music down," I asked Dante. Danny pulled out the money we'd made from last night. We all took out $50,000 a piece for ourselves.

Chapter 7

Danny said that Mr. Johnson had called him earlier about the car wash he had. He wanted to sell it and wanted to see if we were interested in buying it. So we decided to ride by there and check it out.

"Why do you want to get rid of it?" I asked.

"I'm just tired of the complications. I'm an old man with money, but not enough time to enjoy it all. I want to do some traveling also", he said.

We told him that we were very interested, so he took us to see his tax guy who was going to teach me how to handle payroll. He gave us the game, making sure we took care of our business.

Dante and Mark had to take care of some business, so I set up a meeting with our new tax guy for the next day. Mr. Johnson wanted me to ride with him. He said that there was something we needed to discuss. So the guys left and Mr. Johnson and I went to his office, where he sat me down and gave me the whole game about money. He showed me his stock investments, his mutual fund investments, he even showed me how to run his illegal numbers business. He also showed me how he laundered money through his business and he explained to me the system he was using to recycle his dirty cash into clean cash.

After all was said and done, he told me to contact his lawyer, the same one who set up the deal for the store with us, and he would handle everything for us. He dropped me off at the store after we finished working out our business.

As I was about to get out of his car, Mr. Johnson stopped me.

"Billy, good luck with what you and your partners are doing. I did not think you'd last this long, but you did and that is rare. Set your goals, achieve them and then get out," he said.

"I will," I replied. Mr. Johnson was definitely true to the game. He never asked how we made our money, he was from the old school, where he was taught to stay out of people's business.

When I walked into the store, I saw that Ashlee was there. She wanted to go out to eat, but I had homework to do, plus all of the things that Mr. Johnson had told me were on my mind, so I asked her to take me home.

As she was driving me home, she asked me was I going to Miami with her and Jalfanine. I told her that I would let her know tomorrow. I asked her if she would like to go to church with me this coming Sunday. She said that she would love to go.

When Sunday came, Ashlee pulled up to the house in her mother's Cadillac Escalade.

"Park it and come on in," I told her.

My grandmother had met Ashlee earlier and she liked her very much. In fact, she said that we looked very good together and that we made a nice couple.

The church van pulled up to our house and I told Ashlee that we were going to ride with the people in the van, so we went out and got in the van.

"Ashlee, when can I meet your mother?" my grandmother asked Ashlee.

"Soon as you like," Ashlee replied respectfully.

At the church Ashlee was amazed at all the people from school and how nice the people were. She could tell that they did not know about what I was into or what I did. I did not show it either. I had no expensive jewelry, no flashy clothes; I was just Billy.

Ashlee just watched me at church that day. Perhaps she thought it was some type of game or something. She always saw me at school, she saw my commitment to doing my homework and she knew I had plans, but I had not revealed it all to her yet. She was really astonished by this, because I had never allowed her to see this part of me. After church, she asked my grandmother, "Could I please take you out to eat?"

"Of course you can," she replied pleasantly.

Ashlee tried to get me to drive, but I politely declined. It was her mother's truck and I was a little self-conscious about driving it. All week long Ashlee had been asking whether I was going to Miami with her and Jalfanine. I knew that she really wanted me to go and I wanted to go, but I was not about to give her what she wanted that easily. Finally, I said yes and she was so happy.

I gave Ashlee $2,000 to go shopping for me and I told her to keep my things at her house. I also had to go and pick up Jalfanine and give her an envelope from Marco. It had $ 2,500 in it for her to go shopping; she could not believe it. Marco said that he would pick us up.

Danny had been asking me when it was going to go down again. I told him just as soon as I got back, it should be going down, but I told him that it could be as late as Tuesday.

That Friday afternoon, Marco picked us up in his Lincoln Navigator. We talked all the way to Florida. We were headed to his house on the beach. Marco had a beautiful house there.

Marco and Jalfanine were also hitting it off good, because as soon as we hit the door, he was all over Jalfanine and she was loving it. Attached to Marco's house was a four car garage, and in it, he had a Rolls-Royce, a 600 two door Mercedes and a Porsche Cayenne, the new truck. After showing us around the place, he told us all to get dressed, because we were going to his club.

"Baby, I got something special for you to wear tonight," Ashlee purred into my ear as we were heading to get showered and dressed.

"Let me see what you got, Ashlee."

Ashlee blew my mind. She pulled out a $2,000 Armani suit and a pair of $1,500 gator skin shoes! She must have spent about $6,000 to $7,000 on me. I was a nice dresser, but the stuff she'd bought took me to a whole new level of fashion sense. In addition to the clothes, she also had a Movado watch and ring. She had me laced all the way down to my underwear. She was definitely one to try and understand. The club was not far from Marco's house. Once we got there, one of the Cuban guys I met earlier was there to meet us. Inside, we were having a great time. Ashlee and Jalfanine were drinking Cristal and the Cuban guys were talking more English. Ashlee knew a lot of people and everyone seemed to love her.

The next morning, when I awoke, I heard two people talking in Spanish. It was Ashlee and an older woman. Ashlee saw me and came to see what I needed. She said Marco and Jalfanine were out on the beach walking. The Spanish woman she was talking to, was the cook. When Marco and Jalfanine returned, Marco asked Ashlee to take Jalfanine shopping, because he had some business to take care of at the club, plus he wanted me to go with him, but Ashlee immediately objected, saying that she wanted to show me Miami. Marco conceded and told her that she could drive whatever she wanted. She chose the Rolls-Royce.

Ashlee spent $8,000 on Jalfanine with Marco's credit card like it was water, as we viewed Miami like tourists.

Chapter 8

Our plans were to fly back to Nashville, so I called Danny to see if he could pick us up at the airport. I also told him to get Dante's truck, because the girls had bought up Miami! When Danny picked us up, I told him it would be Tuesday and to have everything ready. Danny asked me to drop him off at his girl's house and call Dante if I did not want to keep the truck.

After we dropped off Danny, we dropped Jalfanine off at her house. I called Dante to meet him. Ashlee's car was at the car wash, so I would meet him there. Dante showed up with his girl, but just left his truck at the car wash.

I told Ashlee to drop me off and that I would see her in the morning. I also thanked her for a great time in Miami.

That night I went into my room and thought about all of the things Mr. Johnson had told me about the game of money and how it should be played.

After school the next day, I dropped Ashlee and Jalfanine at the beauty shop and I went to the lawyer Mr. Johnson was telling me about. His name was Mr. Tanner. After talking for a while and determining what I needed, he set us up for a small corporation. Then he showed me how to set up dummy companies to send money back around to the corporation, disguised as profits. In the corporation we had the store, the lawn service and the car wash. He added a house and an office cleaning business. Then he asked me who our tax guy was.

"Mr. Hayes," I said.

He said that Mr. Hayes was a good man. He told me that once we get the money rolling, he would do our investments. I told him that I would go by the banks on Wednesday to set up the bank accounts. As

I was leaving Mr. Tanner's office, Ashlee called me and said they were ready. She said Marco had called and asked where I was.

The next day Ashlee dropped me off at the store, she said she would call me later. Around 6:00pm, she called and asked where I was. I told her I was with Danny looking at an apartment. She asked me to meet her at the store in 30 minutes. I said okay.

Ashlee and Jalfanine pulled up. Ashlee was driving a black truck. She got out, handed me the keys, and told me that they were in the back. We pulled the truck to the back of the store.

Danny already had Mack's money for 30 kilos. Danny called Dante and Mark and told them that we were ready to deal. By 12 o'clock, we were through with the 100 kilos and just like the last time, we kept $50,000 apiece.

I called Ashlee and asked her to come on over; she was there in about 10 minutes. I gave her the keys to the black truck and she was gone. That morning when Ashlee arrived to take me to school, I told her I needed to use the car; I had some business to take care of.

I dropped Ashlee off at school and I went and picked up Mr. Johnson. That day we went to 5 different banks, opened 5 different accounts. I put $3,000 in each account. This was the money game. I would just write checks from one account to another; from the store to the corporation, for the corporation from investments, like AT&T or Microsoft. You name it, we were gonna have stock in it. This was the money game. I could run $50,000 a month through this dummy company and that was like $600,000 a year! That day I learned a lot from Mr. Johnson. He told me to keep my taxes paid and I would have no trouble.

When I dropped him off, I thanked him and asked him if he would allow me to take him to dinner sometime. He said he would love to go, so I told him that I would let him know.

I picked up Ashlee from school, and as we were riding, she told me she had an apartment.

"It's a nice apartment," she said.

"Does your mother know about it?" I asked her.

"No," she said. "And don't you tell her," she added.

I was a little mad, but then it was a nice place, so I just kicked back and enjoyed myself. A little later, Jalfanine came in. I had to take a second look, she was looking so good. I could see what Marco was seeing.

As we were leaving, I saw a new car. I thought Ashlee had bought another car. She saw me looking.

"That's not mines," she said, reading my mind.

"No? Whose is it?"

"Jalfanine's. Marco bought it for her," she said.

It was a Volvo convertible, very nice. I was very surprised by it. As we were getting into Ashlee's car, her cell phone began to ring. It was Marco.

"He wants to speak to you." she handed me the phone.

"Billy, I'm about 20 minutes from you. Can you wait there for me? I need to talk to you."

"Yeah, I'll be here."

Marco pulled up about 20 minutes later in a Mustang. "Hop in, Billy."

Once I got in, he got straight to the point.

"I want to send you some more kilos. Can you handle 500 a month?"

"I will have to talk to my man. How long are you planning to be in town?" I asked.

"I just came to get Jalfanine that ride and get the apartment. I'm flying out tonight."

I told him that I would call him back in an hour. I called Danny and ask him to meet me at the store.

"Billy, I'm at the car wash. Can you meet me there?"

"Yeah, I'm on my way."

When I got there, I told Danny about the proposition to get more product to us.

"Man, that's what Mack has been waiting for. He says that he has business all up in Cincinnati and Indianapolis. Hell, he probably could move 500 himself," he said.

So we decided to take the deal and see if we can have them delivered to Cincinnati and Indianapolis. I called Marco and asked him to meet me real quick. He said he could. Marco said that he could put the dope on the moon if we can sell them.

So Danny made a deal with Mack. He'd let Mack know when he would be in Cincinnati and Indianapolis and we would transact the sales like that. Mack agreed, so it was on.

In one week, I had the money game down! I would make cash deposits through the drive-thru at the bank, then write a check from the dummy company to the corporation. I was getting good, but it was a lot of work.

I learned through Ashlee that Jalfanine was going to Miami almost every weekend. I was happy for her too.

It was getting real close to graduation time and we were all thinking about what we were going to do with our lives. Ashlee was talking about going to Fisk University, but she was still undecided about what she would major in. I'd made up my mind that I was going to T.S.U. to study business.

The annual senior trip was coming up and of all the places to go this year, the senior class decided to go to Miami! I just laughed because I could see how happy Jalfanine and Ashlee were to be going back to Miami so soon. The school was going to charter a bus for us and it would be leaving on Friday night and returning on
Monday night. They were also planning to stop over in Chattanooga to visit the Aquarium.

We talked about it and came to the conclusion that we would be going, but Ashlee wanted to fly.

"No," I said, "what is a senior trip if you do not ride the bus with the rest of your peers?" as I knew she would, she agreed.

Danny, Mark and Dante also decided that they were coming to Miami also, but because they were not in school anymore, they were going to fly down together and meet us. But soon after, they decided to rent a custom bus.

"Billy, we can ride with them," Ashlee suggested after she'd heard they were coming.

"No, we are riding with the bus," I announced.

When we got to Miami, we stayed at the Holiday Inn with everybody else. Danny and them stayed at the Marriott Suites up the street and they had the custom bus parked right out front. Jalfanine stayed out at Marco's house.

Marco and I had talked and he didn't want to meet any of the crew, and I respected that. Ashlee wanted to take Danny, Dante and Mark by the club, but I strongly objected to her suggestion.

"Everything is not for everybody to know."

It was not that I did not trust them, that's just how it is. She then asked me if she could take them shopping in the Rolls-Royce. "No, I said. "But you can take them in the Navigator." I think that Ashlee understood and did not protest.

She showed them Miami and they loved it! As always, she was the perfect hostess. Ashlee knew what they wanted to see and all the things that they'd heard about Miami and before they could request a place, she was already taking them there.

"Thank you," Ashlee said, giving me a kiss.

"What was that for?" I asked.

"For showing me that it's not about showing people what you have. It's about knowing how to handle it and you taught me that this weekend."

"Billy, you should be receiving a package in the mail at the store by Wednesday," she told me after we were back in Nashville.

When Wednesday came, I was at the store to pick up the package when it arrived. It was a box with two remote controls in it to a two-car garage, and the address inside the package was to a house in Indianapolis and Cincinnati. I just put them up.

That weekend, Marco came up to Nashville and took us all out to dinner. He said that since graduation was coming up next week, as a gift he was taking Jalfanine to Las Vegas. If we wanted to go, he had tickets on hold for me and Ashlee. I couldn't say no.

After dinner, Marco and I talked for a while.

"When you get to Indianapolis, just go to the address and use the remote control. Inside of the garage, there will be a van," he alerted me.

"Another thing Billy," he said with curiosity, "What are you doing with your money, if you don't mind me asking," he said politely.

"Ashlee told me you don't even have a car," he added, with a measure of respect in his voice.

I told him about the money game and he liked it, but said he had a better one.

"For 25% of every $100,000, my people will take your money out of the country and deposit it in a bank in the Bahamas. There they will set up an international corporation through which the corporation can set up smaller subsidiaries, such as oil companies and shipping companies. And for an extra 10%, they will funnel your money back to you through banks in New York, where every day they deal with billions of dollars and in this way the Government never sees your money come back into the States," he said. It sounded very sweet.

"So for every 1,000,000 I spend, it will take $300,000 for me to get the $700,000 balance back in the U.S. and spendable," I said.

"Think about this. $700,000 in the bank will buy you a lot more than $1,000,000 on the streets."

"When can we set it up?" I asked eagerly.

"After we come back from Las Vegas."

"Will it be okay if I send you the money on the next trip?"

"Yes, and I guarantee the money will get there," he promised.

As we left, he said that Ashlee would meet me at the store. I called Danny and he said that he already had Mack's money for 35 kilos. I told him I would meet him at the store.

Ashlee pulled up about 20 minutes after I had gotten there, handed me the keys to the van and left with Jalfanine. Danny called Mark and Dante and they all went to work.

About four hours later Ashlee returned to the store to tell me that the other kilos were here. I told Danny to tell Mack that they were there. Mack could not believe that we had it like that. He said he would be leaving out tonight. Danny said he would be there tomorrow. Danny took Dante with him, they were gone about two weeks. I talked to them every day and it seemed to me that they were having fun. After all, the dope was gone and they had sent all the money back except for about $6,000 they had spent shopping.

A few days later me, Marco, Jalfanine and Ashlee were in Las Vegas. Marco was well known at the Mirage Hotel where we stayed. He had us on the top floor in the suites, the size of houses. These suites had to cost Marco around $2,000 a night; but later Marco said that the rooms and the plane tickets were free. Marco also kept $4,000 in the hotel on tab just for gambling or whatever his pleasure.

I loved Las Vegas. It was a place made of dreams and since school was out and I was now a graduate about to begin his first stint at college, I carefully allowed myself the opportunity to enjoy some of the luxuries I could afford.

Chapter 9

I bought me a brand new Maxima. Danny bought a house for him and his girl, because she was about to have a baby. through the corporation that Mr. Tanner had set up for me, A few weeks later, Marco, me and the girls flew down to the Bahamas. They thought it was for fun, but in actuality it was for business. I met a man named Mr. Wolf at the Bahama National Bank and he explained how the account was to be set up.

"I'm going to need a name first," he said, as if we were doing the most legitimate business.

"Bill Contour," I said, just coming from the top of my head. "Give me another name?" he said laughing, "Bill has trouble." "Robert Ruth," I replied.

"Alright," he said, enthused.

"The corporation's books will be in this name and you will have access to this money in that name. All the taxes will be paid in that name also. Now the name that owns the company will be William Chandler. These papers you do not let anyone see. No one," he said seriously.

"So no one will know that I own this corporation, but you and me?" I asked.

"Yes," he replied. "It will be kept on file here, however, the only way anyone can look into these files is with your presence available," he said.

He said that anytime I wanted to move some money into my account, just let him know.

"Most people start moving money after about 3 months, because you must remember that we are taking this slow," he paused for a moment.

"I see that you already have another corporation. Well, we can link them together, but I would advise you to keep them separate. That way if anything happens to one, the other will be safe."

After signing all of the paperwork, I thanked Mr. Wolf, and he told Marco to tell Ashlee to call him. When we left the Bahamas, we went to Miami. Marco was opening a woman's boutique, and Ashlee was hard at work helping him to get it all together.

I really needed to get back to Nashville, so I told her to stay and finish what she had started and I would go back. Before she hung up, she asked if I would like to go to a fashion show in Paris and Italy. I was definitely game, so she told me to go to the post office and get a passport.

Marco, Ashlee and Jalfanine returned to Nashville the following Thursday. I picked them up from the airport and drove them back to Ashlee's apartment. Marco wanted to talk.

"Can your man Danny handle everything while we are out of the country?" he asked, looking to me for an answer.

"No doubt," I said, knowing full well that Danny was more than capable of this task.

I called Danny and told him of everything that was going on. He was shocked when I told him I was going to Paris.

"Damn nigga, I know I said live it up, but damn you're taking this shit to a whole new level!" he said, laughing like hell.

"How long will you be gone?"

"About two weeks."

The flight to Paris was amazingly long, but short compared to any other means of travel. I'd never really seen the world from this particular view and my appreciation for it grew immensely.

While we were in Paris, Ashlee said that there was something that she needed to talk to me about. At first, she acted like whatever she was trying to say was hard, but to me this was much unlike the Ashlee that I knew. She decided that we would talk later.

At the fashion show, Ashlee worked her ass off! As I watched her handling her business, I said to myself that she was surely meant for this business. And Jalfanine was doing a good job herself.

As we left Paris, Ashlee poured herself into ordering things for the store, so we never got around to talking about whatever was on her mind.

In Italy, she opened up, speaking Italian like it was her first language. Even Jalfanine was shocked. Ashlee said that this store was going to be one of the best and exclusive places in Miami that anyone had ever seen, and she was going to make it happen. I believed her.

I had not talked to Danny in about a week or so. When I finally had a chance to talk to him, he said that there had been a little trouble, but that we could talk about it when I returned.

"When you get back, we can talk about it then," he said.

"No shit; have fun", he had everything under control. When we were on the plane coming home, I finally asked Ashlee about the topic that she said we needed to discuss.

"So what is it that you want to talk with me about Ashlee?" I asked her.

"It's nothing," she said, giving me a kiss and going back to ordering for the store.

We changed planes in New York. I headed to Nashville and they went on to Miami. Ashlee said that she would call me and that she would be home by Wednesday.

"Will you pick me and Jalfanine up?" she asked me sweetly.

"Of course I will," I replied.

Once I was back in Nashville, at the airport Danny and Dante were there to pick me up. The news was that Mark had gotten caught with 2 kilos. The police pulled him over for speeding, they said; plus Mark had no driver's license on him. The police searched the car and found the drugs. Mark's mother and grandmother put up their house to get him out.

"When did this happen?"

"About three days ago," Danny said.

"Does he have a lawyer yet?" I asked.

Danny didn't know because he hadn't talked to him, he had just gotten out yesterday. So we called him and planned to meet at a restaurant. Mark showed up about 15 minutes after we did. He did not seem bothered by what had happen, but I was. After he told me what happened, we talked about getting him the best lawyer we could find. We ate and laughed, as they asked me all about my trip to Paris and Italy. I told them that just me and Ashlee went.

The next day I called Mr. Tanner and he gave me the name of a lawyer that he said could take care of everything. His name was Mr. Goodwin.

I called Mr. Goodwin and set up a meeting with him for Mark, but I was going too, so we could see what was going on.

After talking to Mr. Goodwin, he said that he could beat the case. The police did not give Mark a ticket for speeding, so why did they stop him? Even though he stopped Mark and found drugs, there is no evidence to support his reason for stopping him.

"He can't come a week later and issue a ticket, do you see where I am going with all of this?" he asked.

He told Mark not to worry about anything, he would take care of this with no problem.

"So how much is this going to cost us?" I asked.

"$15,000 to start, and $400 an hour for any court appearances after the probable cause hearing, but I guarantee that we won't get that far," he reassured us.

I wrote him a check.

"Mark, you've got to keep your nose clean, because the courts are backed up. It is going to take about 5-6 months to straighten this out, so stay clean," he warned.

We thanked him and we left. Mark was in his Navigator, they had taken his S.S.; Mark said he should have asked about his car.

"You can call him tomorrow about that," I said.

As soon as they left, I got a call from Ashlee.
"Is everything alright?" she asked.

"Yeah, everything is cool," I said.

"Jalfanine told me about what happened with Mark and she said he was set up," she said.

"Nah, he just got pulled over by the police and he had no license."

"You sure baby?"

"Yeah, I'm positive. We just left the lawyer's office; he said everything will be okay. So, how is everything going with the store?"

"We are waiting for the orders to come in, but I will be coming home tomorrow. My mother wants me to go to this meeting with her," she said. "And she wants me to register for college. Can you pick me up? My plane will be in at 2pm."

I told her yes, I'll be there. Mark had to lay low, so when we handled business, we made sure he got everything he needed.
Things were still going well, as far as our work in Cincinnati and Indianapolis was concerned. Danny's girl had a baby boy and he was hyped about that. I was happy for him. When Ashlee came home from Miami, she bought the baby so much stuff, I could not believe it! She actually went crazy over that baby. I guess it was because she was an only child.

As we left Danny's house, we talked about the store in Miami.

"Are you coming to the grand opening? I've already got your clothes together."

"If everything goes as smoothly as I plan for it to, you know I will be there to support you," I replied.

I could see that Ashlee wanted to say something, but she did not seem to know how to express it.

"Ashlee, are you alright?"

"Yes," she said, sitting there looking slightly distracted and agitated.

"Are you sure?" I asked.

I knew this was not her. Then she started to cry, not bawling or anything like that but the tears were flowing and her chest slowly heaved in sharp but silent gasps. Slowly she grabbed my hand and squeezed it. I was not sure what was going on, but I figured that whatever was on her mind, any minute now she'd be ready to talk. So I pulled into the park.

"Ashlee baby, what's wrong?" I asked "It's

because of you," she sighed.

I did not understand though. Ashlee launched into a thing about her and me. She said that she could not get me out of her mind.

"I don't know what it is, and to this day I can't figure it out," she said, smiling through her tears.

"Billy, I first hooked up with you as a way to make some extra money here in Nashville, but the more I saw of you, the more I began to feel," she said.

She said that she was observing me looking for my angle in life, a motive for doing what I did. And the motive was usually selfish and self-centered. So she was thinking at first that I was just a smooth guy, then we went to Atlanta and I met George and Marco. "Who is George?" I asked curiously.

"He's the Cuban guy that did most of the talking that first night," she said.

"Billy, I hope that you won't be mad with me, but at this point I have to tell you the truth."

"What's up?" I asked her, waiting on her to drop a bomb on me.

"George used to be my boyfriend until I found him messing with my best friend. Well, I cannot call her a friend," she said, adding, "I knew all along what George and his family did so we shrugged a deal. Whatever deal we set, he would make sure that I get my cut and that's where Marco comes in. His mother blames me for Marco being a drug dealer. You see, I brought Marco in to handle all the business that I bring in and he and I split the profits 60/40, 60 my way and 40 Marco's way.

"I ended up here in Nashville because my mother wanted to get out of Miami, so my father transferred here to Nashville. When we were in Atlanta, I was putting up a fight for you, so I told George that every shipment that he sent you, I would back. That's why he sent you 100 kilos. No other time has he sent that many, but you came through like no one imagined you could. You showed them and you showed me that you are as good as your word, and in this business that is very hard to find."

"At first, I thought that would be it, but the more I hang around you, the more I came to see what you were all about, and I like what I saw tremendously. Billy, of all the cars you could have bought, you bought a Maxima. I know that you can afford a better vehicle than that, but your moderation is your strength. When we went to Miami, you saw the danger of letting even your friends know what you were dealing with. And on that trip, you stayed with the senior class when you could have probably paid for the best hotel in Miami, no problem. These are the things that I have come to love in you and this is why I am confiding in you, and I will truthfully answer any question you ask because I do not want any more lies between us, on my account."

"What about the store and the night club in Miami?" I asked.

"The store in Miami is mine, 100%," she said, staring at me directly in the eyes for the first time tonight.

"Marco and George, they have nothing to do with it. The club is a little different, I own 30%, Marco owns 30% and George owns the last 40%." she said.

"Anything else I should know about?"

"Billy, I bought Jalfanine's car for her. Marco thought that she was definitely someone nice to kick it around with and he was not trying to get too serious. Plus, when I met Jalfanine, she was getting out of a bad relationship and I wanted to see her get her self-esteem back, and do some positive things with her life. Jalfanine never once asked me about my business and she say that we make a beautiful couple. She can't wait to see us five years from now," she said, smiling my way.

"When we went to the Bahamas, I was the one who set that up, Marco had nothing to do with it. I talked to Mr. Wolf right after you left. I told him to give your account the same treatment he gives mine. Bill, I am telling you all of this because I am pregnant." "Pregnant?" I asked, surprised and feeling light. I just froze. I didn't know if I should be happy, I knew I was scared. "How many months along are you?" "About two months," Ashlee said.

I'd never seen her have this much difficulty expressing anything, so I knew this was killing her.

"Are we about to be parents?" I asked her seriously.

"It is up to you," she said, looking over at me.

"Do we buy the house in Nashville or Miami?" I asked, to lighten the mood.

She leaned over and gave me a kiss.

"I thought you would be upset," she said.

"No, we both did this. I can't just blame you."

"What about school?"

"I plan on sitting out this year, but Billy, you should still go. We have a family to raise."

"When are you going to tell your family?" I asked her.

"We'll tell them next week, after the opening of the store."

After our talk, we left the park and went to get something to eat. This was gonna be a long night for us. Later that night, I told her to drop me off at the store, making sure she was alright before I let her drive off. I could tell she was happy, so I gave her a kiss to seal the bond we'd made tonight.

Chapter 10

Danny called and said Mack was in town and he wanted to know what was up. I told him to meet me at the car wash. Right after that, Ashlee called and said that she had a van for me and she was leaving out tonight to go back to Miami.

"Can you drop it off at the store?" I asked her.
"Give the keys to Mrs. Parker," I added.
"Alright," she said.

I met Danny at the car wash and told him it would be at the store in about 30 minutes. Dante pulled up with Mark in the truck. Mark said everything was going good and that Mr. Goodwin would have his car back to him by Friday. Mark and Dante were about to go to get something to eat, and asked did we want to go. I told him we had some business to take care of. Mark asked if we needed his help.
"Mark, you need to lay low," I stated.
"If you need anything, we got you. What, your money running low?"
"Billy, I just miss the game," he said.
It was fun for Mark. Personally, I never thought selling drugs was fun. I thought it was business and I always looked at it that way.
Danny left to go get Mack's money. Dante jumped in the car with me. I called the store and I asked Mrs. Parker to stay at the store for a few minutes longer and I would be there soon. I took Dante to get his car, and while we were riding, he was calling all of his people and letting

them know that he was back in business. I dropped him off and he said that he would be at the store in 20 minutes.

"Bet," I said.

Hours later, we had finished getting rid of the product. Ashlee came by to get the van.

"Bill, will you take me and Jalfanine to the airport?" she asked me.

"What time?" I asked.

"Well, our plane leaves at 9:45," she said.

I picked them up at their apartment, where Ashlee gave me my plane ticket.

"The opening is Thursday and it will last all weekend," she reminded me.

I dropped them both off at the airport, and I told them that I would see them Thursday. As they were leaving, Ashlee turned quickly and returned to the car.

"I already have your clothes packed, so don't worry about what you will wear," she said, smiling and giving me a kiss.

As I watched Ashlee walking away from me, I could not help but say to myself, "This is the girl that I am going to spend the rest of my life with."

Thursday, my plane left at 1:00pm. I called Danny, but his phone just rang, so I hung up. A few minutes later, he called.

"I was going to get you to drop me off at the airport, but it's alright. I will just park in the long term parking. I will call you tonight, alright?"

"Okay, that's cool," he said.

"How is the baby?" I asked.

"He's okay," he said.

When I got to Miami, I looked for Ashlee. She always met me coming off the plane. As I walked into the airport lobby, I saw this guy with a sign over his head that said William Chandler. As I got closer, I said to him, "I'm William Chandler."

"I'm your driver for today. Ms. Boycess said you should call her once you're in the car."

Once we were in the car, he turned on the phone.

"Hello? Ms. Boycess speaking." It was Ashlee.

"How are you Ms. Boycess," I said.

"Baby, I hope the flight was alright. I am here at the club getting ready for the fashion show tonight. I will be at the hotel tonight around 7:00pm," she said.

"Where are my clothes for tonight?" I asked Ashlee.

"They're in the closet. If you are hungry, order room service. We might not have time to go out to eat. I love you, and if you need anything, you know how to reach me," she said, hanging up before I ever responded.

When we arrived at the hotel, in the lobby was a picture of Ashlee's store. The sign read, "Fashion Miami. Welcome." The driver picked up my keys to the room and gave me a red beeper with a button.

"If you need transportation, just push the button and I will be here in a matter of minutes," he said.

I tipped him and thanked him. When I went up to my room, I was surprised, because it was bigger than any suite I had ever seen. It was the size of a house! I took off my clothes and relaxed.

The phone rang; it was Ashlee.

"Billy, be ready to leave at 6:30. The fashion show starts at 8:00, but I will be there to ride with you at 7:00. I love you," she said, hanging up quickly again.

When we arrived at the club, I could not believe all of the limos in front of the club.

"Wait until you see the inside," she said.

The front had the red carpet rolled out and there were spotlights illuminating the area like we were in Hollywood or something. Ashlee had the inside fixed up like a castle; it was beautiful. As we made our way in, I could see all of the designers that Ashlee had worked with. Ashlee was moving through the crowd with grace, talking in French and Italian. She was greeting everyone with love, and the show was a huge success.

At the end of the fashion show, they called her up on stage and the audience gave her a huge hand. Ashley was so drained that she actually fell asleep on the way back to the hotel.

By 8 o'clock the next morning, Ashlee was up again. She had one more event to take care of before opening the store. She had this mapped out; tonight there was an art show at the museum in downtown Miami, sponsored by Fashion Miami and Christies. This was a black tie affair.

That afternoon, I called Danny to see if everything was going smooth. He said that all was fine, so I told him that I would be checking back with him later.

The art show was a very elegant affair and we had a great time there also. The grand opening was Saturday. I told Ashlee I would be there around 2pm.

When I arrived, there were people everywhere. The news reporters had covered the fashion show and the art show so people everywhere already knew about the grand opening of Fashion Miami.

Jalfanine was running around trying to make sure that everyone was where they were supposed to be. I could see that Ashlee had a winner here. Ashlee could not see me, because of all the people surrounding her, but after a few minutes or so she found me and came right over. She began by showing me the place. She took me to her office and while we were there, she told me how tired she was, but that she was happy about how things turned out. A few minutes later, Marco came in and he and I talked for a while as Ashlee went to handle some business.

"Billy, we are throwing Ashlee a surprise party tonight, so when this is all over we need the two of you to come by the club. Can you handle it?" he asked.

"You know I can," I said.

The store closed at 8 o'clock and there were still people trying to get in. Ashlee, being the business woman she was, dealt with them all. We did not leave until about 9:30pm. Ashlee was dead tired.

I beeped the driver and he showed up in 10 minutes.

"We gotta go out tonight and celebrate," I said energized.

"Okay, baby," she said, but I could see how tired she really was.

I told the driver to head to the club.

"Why the club?" she asked.

"Because that's where I want to go, sweetheart," I said smoothly. When we walked into the club, the whole place went crazy! Everybody was congratulating her and giving her hugs. Marco gave her a dozen roses. We had a wonderful time.

Around 2am, Ashlee was so tired that I told Marco we had to go. We thanked everyone and we left. When we got back to the hotel, there was a message for me to call Danny.

"I'll call him in the morning, 'cause it's too late, I replied.

"Maybe you should call him now," she said, turning over sleepily and mumbling.

"If he is calling this late, it could be important."

So I decided to call, and discovered that Dante was at the hospital. He had been shot by someone who had tried to rob him.

"He got shot in the shoulder and the leg," Danny said. He sounded frustrated.

"He didn't wanna give it up."

"Danny, I will be home the first flight out."

Ashlee over heard the conversation and she was up, wide awake. I told her not to worry about it, but that I would be needing her to get me a flight back to Nashville first thing in the morning. She got on the phone as soon as I hung up the phone with Danny and had me a ticket for the next flight out, which would be that morning at 9am.

"Do you want me to come with you?" Ashlee asked.

"No, I will be okay. You just handle your business down here," I said, holding her to me gently that night, wondering what the morning would bring.

Chapter 11

I waited patiently for my flight to leave. I was on pins and needles all morning long. The next morning, Ashlee took me to the airport, where I waited patiently for my flight to leave. When I finally reached Nashville, Danny met me in the lobby of the airport.

"What's up?" I asked him. "How's Dante?"

"He was hit by one bullet in the main artery of his shoulder. At first they couldn't stop the bleeding, but it is cool now. The other bullet went straight through his leg," Danny said, as we exited the airport, heading to the hospital.

When we got there, Dante was housed on the fifth floor. As we carefully entered the room, I saw that Dante's mother was there. I had never met her before, so I politely introduced myself, then went to Dante and gave him a hug.

"How are you feeling?" I asked him.

"I'm feeling a lot better than I was last night," he said, wincing with a little discomfort.

"The doctor says I will survive."

"How long have you been here, Mark?" I asked Mark, who was also there.

"All night long," he said.

Dante's mother had to leave.

"Dante, if you need anything, you just call me. I will be back this afternoon," she said, giving him a kiss on the cheek, saying goodbye to us all.

Dante's girl was there too, but she also had to leave. She reminded him about all the girls that kept calling and coming by. She said they will talk about that another time. She kissed him and left.

A few minutes later, the nurse came in and checked Dante's shoulder for bleeding, and said that he may be able to leave tomorrow. As soon as she left and we knew that we had some privacy, Dante went into what had happened.

He said that he had stopped by the store to get some snacks. As he was pulling into the parking lot, he saw a car that looked like it was following him, but he said he just played it off. Then, as he was leaving the store, he saw the car again; but this time it was going the other way, so he went on home.

"After I got home," Dante was saying, "I called Kim to tell her to come over, and suddenly someone was kicking in my door! I hadn't been in the apartment 20 minutes. They had on masks, but I think I know who it was. I'm just gonna wait to see that car again and when I do, it's on man!" Dante paused.

"They tried to kill me."

"What did they take from you?" I asked.

"They got my Rolex, a platinum chain, about $10,000 and the keys to my truck," he said.

"When we find out who did this shit, they're gonna pay!" Mark said, jumping up in a fury.

"No, think about it. This has got to be handled in a better way," I said, trying to bring an element of calmness to this situation.

"Mark, you already have enough trouble."

Deep in my heart, I knew that they were gonna handle it and nothing I said was going to change that. A few minutes later, the nurse came in and told us that we would have to leave. The doctor was on his way, and we would have to return in about an hour if we wanted to spend any more time with Dante.

"Hey Mark, me and Danny are gonna go and get something to eat, do you wanna ride?" I asked him as we were about to leave the hospital.

"Naw. I got some riding to do."

"Mark, don't get into any trouble. You've got to lay low. We can handle this in some other way, guns will bring in the police and we don't need that."

"I understand, I'm just gonna ride," he said.

"Hey Billy," Danny said as we were riding to get some food.

"You know that as soon as Dante finds out who did this to him, it's gonna be on. And to be honest with you, I might feel the same way if it happened to me."

"But Danny, you have to play it smart."

"But letting dudes stick you up and walk away is not a very bright idea either," he said.

"If you look at it, it's part of the game. If you play football, you are likely to get hurt. If you sell drugs, you're likely to get robbed or shot, so you have to be on guard at all times, because you are a target. Dante saw the car and could have prevented this from happening, but he did not control the situation. It's a lesson," I said.

"A lesson, huh? Billy, don't be naive to this game. It ain't all brains, it's muscle too," he said.

After eating, Danny took me back to the car.

"I'll see you later," I told him.

The next day, I went by the hospital to see Dante, but the nurse said he had been released. He was staying at his mother's house for the time being. So I drove over there to check up on him.

"I know who it was," Mark said, who was also there.

"My boy seen big G with Dante's Rolex on, and the car you saw was big G's girl's car. Now I know where this clown lives, but because you asked us to lay low, we are," Mark said.

His eyes were dancing crazily in his head.

"Let it go for now, because we don't need the police on our backs", I said.

My phone rang. It was Danny and he said he needed to talk and could I meet him at the car wash.

"It's important," he said,

As I left, I told Dante and Mark to be cool, get well and everything would be alright. When I got to the car wash, Danny was already there. As soon as he saw me, he jumped in the car.

"Mack made the news in Indiana. This female I be kickin' it with called and said that on the news they said he has been under investigation for the past ten months by the DEA and FBI. He was caught with 38 kilos and $1.5 million. It's been on the news all day. From what I hear, they have been trying to see if he will talk. She said that he is facing 30 years to life. She told me she would call back if she hears anything else."

"Do you think he will talk?" I asked.

"Billy, with that much time hanging over his head, I just don't know. But I do know this, Mack has been doing time on and off for the last few years. He just beat a gun charge because one of his boys took the charge for him. But to answer your question, I don't know."

"Danny, I believe that we are going to need to take a break," I said, thinking about where things could go from here.

"I need to call Ashlee and see when she will be coming back, but in the meantime, I think that we should get away for a while. Take a trip together."

We rode back over to Dante's mother's house to see what they thought about taking a trip. Dante was with it, but he said that he needed to talk with his doctor. Mark was with it too, but he wanted to talk with Mr. Goodwin, his lawyer, to make sure it was okay for him to go.

I called Ashlee and explained to her that everything would have to slow down and that we were all planning on taking a trip, possibly to California.

"Can I go with you?" she asked.

"But what about the store?" I asked her.

"Jalfanine can handle it," Ashlee said. "She is my manager anyway."

"Dante checking with his doctor to see if he can go. It is going to be about two weeks before we actually leave anyway."

"Baby, I love you and I am flying in Friday to see you. Be careful, alright? Give Dante my prayers," she said.

"That's cool," I said, and we hung up.

Everything was going according to schedule. Mark and Dante both had to go ahead and travel, so I had Ashlee set up traveling arrangements. We were scheduled to leave in a couple of days, so that was cool. Everyone was also going to take their girls with them.

A couple of days before we were scheduled to leave, Danny's girl in Indiana called again and said that a guy by the name of K-L, had set Mack up. She also said that there were 35 other people on Mack's case with federal indictments on them.

The word had also gotten back to big G. He said that he had bought the Rolex, and that if Dante wanted it back, he could buy it from him. I told Dante not to sweat it.

"We are going on a vacation. Let's leave all this drama behind us until we get back," I advised him.

We stayed in California for a week. We stayed in L.A., but we traveled everywhere we could think about. It was a beautiful vacation. I wished we could have stayed there forever.

Chapter 12

On the plane ride back home, I sat with Dante.

"Dante, I know you man, and I can see that you have something up. But think about the trouble it could bring. It's not worth it," I said. "You have too much to lose. Big G's broke, man. That's what made him do that. Don't do it, please, we don't need the trouble. I will replace everything they took from you Dante, but you've got to give up this thing for us."

"Billy, you can't buy these bullets they put in me, but I will try to, alright? And that is all I can say, because I cannot promise you nothing," Dante said.

I thanked him for that much. Big G was in trouble, and I knew it. When we got back to Nashville, everyone headed home to take the place in life they had reserved before we left for California. Three days later, Ashlee and I were in Miami looking for a house when Danny called me.

"Yo Billy, let me give you the news now before you hear it from someone else," he said.

"What's up Danny?" I could feel my heartbeat in my ears.

"They found Big G dead in his apartment. The police have a suspect, but they are not naming names yet," Danny informed me.

"Have you talked to Dante or Mark?" I asked.

"No, they are not answering their phones."

"Danny, call me back if anything new develops," I said, knowing that this was only the beginning. Danny called back about two hours later.

"They've just flashed Mark and Dante's picture on the news. They are wanted for questioning. But you know what that means, don't you?"

"Yeah," I said.

"But that's not the half of it, Billy. Peep this shit," Danny said.

"Mark has an indictment against him for the sale of 25 kilos of cocaine."

"What!" I was surprised. This was too much too soon. "And they are saying he sold it to an FBI informant." "You've got to find them," I said.

"I will try and I will get back with you," Danny said.

I called Mr. Goodwin, Mark's lawyer, and he said that the FBI had just called him and alerted him of the fact of his client's news problems.

"Billy, if you talk to Mark, tell him the best thing for him to do is to turn himself in. I am headed out right now to get a copy of the indictment. Call me back," he said.

"Alright Mr. Goodwin," I said hanging up. I called him back about an hour later.

"Billy, I have talked to Dante and Mark and they both say that they have nothing to do with it," he said.

"I am arranging a lawyer for Dante. They plan on turning themselves in tomorrow. Now Billy, the indictment on Mark is from the case he just got with the drugs. I think that I can handle it though. Just call me tomorrow."

I told Ashlee about everything that was going down, and that I needed to return to Nashville. Danny met me at the airport. He informed me that a witness claims to have seen Dante and Mark leave from Big G's house in Mark's sister's car, and the witness got the tag number after she heard the shots. "Have you talked to them?" "No," he said.

"I talked to Mr. Goodwin and he wants to meet."

Danny was not down with that so I asked him to run the store for me while I handle this meeting. I met Mr. Goodwin at his office at 9:30 in the morning. He said that he would be recommending Mr. Kaplan, one of his associates to Dante.

"He's one of the best defense lawyers in town," he said.

"What is the deal with Mark?" I asked him.

"He has an indictment which accuses him of being a major player in a huge drug ring, and he was served because of his alleged involvement in a murder," Mr. Goodwin said.

There was a knock at the door and Mr. Kaplan walked in. I introduced myself and asked about what he was prepared to do, but he said he needed to study the case. He said he would know in a couple of days. I wrote Mr. Goodwin a check for $10,000 and I wrote Mr. Kaplan a check for $15,000.

"When you see them, tell them I said for them to keep their heads up."

That night, it was all over the news. I couldn't believe that this was happening to us. They talked a lot about Mark and his indictment. They also said that they took 3 cars, some jewelry, and $150,000 from his apartment. Suddenly the phone rang, it was Danny.

"Are you watching the news?" he asked.

"Yeah man, this shit is getting deep," I said, more to myself than to him.

The next day, I called Mr. Goodwin, and he said that the Feds had about 25 more indictments coming out this week. He said that they also took a footprint from the front door of the apartment where the murder took place, and the print matches the shoe that Mark had on when he turned himself in.

"If the woman who gave the police the tag number on the car comes and identifies them, they will be looking at first degree murder," Mr. Goodwin said, flatly.

He said that G's girlfriend said that he was killed because he was suspected of shooting and robbing Dante, but she says that she doesn't know how he got Dante's watch and that some guy named Mike showed Dante and Mark where Big G lived.

"I am just getting all the facts, so just keep at it and I will keep you informed," he said.

I called Danny and told him about all I had learned. I suggested to him that he should leave for a while. His girl had family in Dallas, Texas, so I told him that they should go there for a couple of weeks. He agreed. I went to Miami with Ashlee.

Marco was nervous about me being down there with all that was going on in Nashville. I assured him that I was not in any trouble and that everything would work out for the best.

Three days later, I called Mr. Goodwin back.

"The government is asking Mark to cut a deal. As we speak, he is facing 30 years to life, and they want to know everything. There are also 7 people willing to testify against him right now," he said. "Right now, he is saying that he can't do it, but his family is putting a lot of pressure on him."

"What are the chances at beating this?" I asked.

"It does not look good. They have him on video and tape. It's very hard to fight against the evidence they have against him. But give me a few days and I may have something positive for you." I called Danny and let him know what was going on.

"Man, Mark might break," he said coldly.

"But it's his word against ours," I said.

At this point, things began to look really bad, and I was wondering if they could get any worse. They did. I received a call from Mr. Goodwin a few days later.

"Billy, Dante has been indicted. Some of the same people that are testifying against Mark have dealt with Dante, and they are trying to indict Mark's girlfriend, because she was present at two of his drug deals. Things are developing rather quickly now," he said.

"Billy, do you have a lawyer?"

"Why?" I asked, thinking of my own connection to Dante and Mark.

"Well, because the FBI has been asking about a William Chandler a.k.a Billy, and a Danny Stephens. Someone is already talking, we just don't know who. Oh, and one more thing."

"What's that?"

"Tell Danny that Mack is cooperating with the Government. Dante sent that message. I talked to his lawyer today. Billy, if you need a good lawyer, call Michael Hawthorne. He can help you," he said, giving me his phone number.

I called Danny and again alerted him to everything that was going on. I also told him that I was getting us a lawyer, so if one calls, just talk to him. "Let's just be prepared if something comes up," I said.
He sounded cool with that. In fact, he sounded quite relaxed, a relaxation I didn't feel. The next day I called Mr. Hawthorne and he said that Mr. Goodwin had told him about me and that he needed to see me as soon as possible, if he was to be of any help to me. I told him I was in Miami and I'll be there tomorrow. Ashlee dropped me off at the airport.
Her stomach was getting big. I told her everything would be alright. She kissed me with tears in her eyes.

"Be strong, I will call you tonight," I said.

"Everything will work out, you'll see."

I arrived at Mr. Hawthorne's office at 9am. He was in a meeting with another lawyer, so I had to wait. Finally, after about 15 minutes, he called me into his office and we talked about my connections with Mark and Dante.

"Did you know they were going to kill this guy called Big G?" he asked.

"No," I said.

"Right now, there is no indictment on you or your friend Danny, but the way that things are going it is a very realistic possibility that you will have some soon. After talking to Dante's lawyer, they are pushing them real hard. The prosecutor is doing all he can to get them to talk. Telling Dante and Mark they're getting life. I am going to refer your friend Danny to a lawyer who had been with us for ten years. His name is Robert Kroner, here is his number," he said, handing me a card.

I wrote him two checks for $10,000 a piece to retain lawyer for us. When I left Mr. Hawthorne's office, I was not feeling too good about things, but I had to check on everything. I went by the car wash and everything there was alright. Then I stopped by the store to check in with Mrs. Parker. She said that the store was doing real good and that everything was going okay.

"Is everything alright with your friends?" she asked.

"Yes Ma'am, they just got into a little trouble," I said, attempting to make light to the situation.

Mark and Dante never handled any of the business operations, it was mostly me and sometimes Danny. I called Danny and told him that I had hired an attorney for him and I gave him the phone number and name of his new lawyer. He asked me had I met him, and I told him no, but he is good from what I heard.

Then I just rode around looking at Nashville, thinking about Ashlee and the baby, knowing that things were about to get bad. The next day, I called Mr. Goodwin, but the conversation was very brief, because he was on his way to see Mark, so I asked him to call me later.

I then called my attorney, Mr. Hawthorne. He said that things were looking bad, but he couldn't be too sure just how bad yet. He was waiting on a call from Mr. Kaplan, Dante's lawyer. He asked me to call him back in about an hour.

Ashlee called about twenty minutes later to announce that she would be coming to Nashville the next day. She said that the store was doing fine and that she had just left a doctor's appointment and the doctor said the baby was a girl.

"I've got pictures and everything," she said cheerfully.

I did not wish to bring her down with my problems, so I pretended not to be distracted, but it took all of my concentration to talk to her. I was under pressure.

After I got off the phone with Ashlee, I drove around for about an hour that seemed like two days, and eventually ended up at Mr. Hawthorne's office. I entered and told his secretary to let him know I was outside. She did.

"Mr. Hawthorne says you should come on back," she said politely.

He met me at the door. He had a sad look on his face and my heart immediately sank.

"What's going on?" I asked.

"Dante has decided to talk," he said.

I was devastated, to say the least. How could Dante do this to us?

"How much information does he have about you and your dealings?" he asked.

"Well," I sighed. "He's seen me with drugs and we have conducted business together; but it is just his word against mine", thinking I had a chance.

"Look, I need to know something and I don't want you to sugar coat this for me either. Did you have anything to do with this murder?" Mr. Hawthorne asked me seriously.

"No," I said.

Then the phone rang, it was his secretary. She said that Mr. Kaplan was outside and he wanted to speak with Mr. Hawthorne. I was about to leave when Mr. Kaplan asked me to stay.

"Mr. Chandler, I tried to talk Dante out of working with the Government, but his girlfriend and his family are pushing him to do it, telling him to save himself. The prosecutor kept going to his family and I think that is what did it. He also fired me. He is hiring another lawyer," he said.

"Why did he fire you?" I asked.

"Because he says that I am too close to you," he said. "And I believe that Mark is next."

"If they both turn and work for the Government, from what you've told me, it's just a matter of time before they indict you and Danny. Let me see how we should handle this, and I promise to get back with you."

I immediately left his office and called Danny. He said that he had just got off the phone with Mr. Kroner.

"He says that he was going to visit a client when he saw Mr. Kaplan. Mr. Kaplan told him that Dante had decided to work for the Government."

"So you know about Mack too?" "Yeah,"
he said sourly.

"Is there anything you need?" I asked.

"Yeah, I need for you to drop off another 20 g's to my lawyer. He says that he is going to need it because shit's about to get deeper."

"I got that," I said calmly.

"Danny, what do you think is going to happen, man? I asked.

"I sincerely don't know Billy. Let's just wait and see," he replied.

Danny sent his girl's brother over to his house to collect their clothes and take them to his mother's house and to put the furniture into a storage facility. He told them to leave his cars there, so it would look like he was still there.

I told him to take care and I'll call him later. I headed towards my grandmother's house, but quickly changed my mind. I could not face her just yet, so I dipped over to Ashlee's apartment. When I got there, she was waiting for me. Her face had gotten a cute chubbiness about it and her belly was definitely bulging, and the smile on her face helped me forget about my own troubled mind. I wanted to tell her exactly what was going on, but now things were different, she was living for two and I did not want to upset her in any way at all. I took her to see her mother, and while we were there, I got another disturbing phone call. It was from Mr. Hawthorne. He said that Mark was also going to work for the Government! I told Ashlee that I had to run, but I would be back and that we would go to dinner together later. I flew over to Mr. Hawthorne's office.

When I got to his office, he told me nothing had changed since we last talked, but that Danny and I should just lay low.

"It is only going to be a matter of time before you and Danny are indicted, and if they pick you up, don't make any statements. Just call me," he said. I asked him if I owed him any money, but he told me not to worry about it just yet because nothing had really happened yet.

"Billy, just go on home and relax. If anything changes, I will be sure to notify you. Alright?"

"Okay," I said, knowing that there was very little chance of me doing any relaxing.

Chapter 13

A week went by with no word from Mr. Hawthorne. I was on pins and needles awaiting what I knew was going to occur. I finally decided that I was going to go to Miami and try to relax. It was all I could do.

"Mr. Hawthorne, I am going to Miami for a few days. I cannot relax here. Will it be cool?"

"Yes Billy, just relax," he said.

In Miami, Ashlee and I began looking for a house. After all, we were a family. I called every other day inquiring about any changes in my free status and everything was cool. I called Danny every day, and he said that he was cool. He had been just hanging out with his girlfriend's cousin.

After about a month and a half, I began to think maybe there was nothing to worry about. "Perhaps things are not as bad as I have been making them," I thought to myself. But as usual, I was wrong.

About one week later, I called Danny's place but I didn't get a response. I waited for about three hours, thinking that perhaps he was out shopping or something, then I called him back again and still there was no answer. I tried every number I knew: his apartment number, his cell phone number, even his girlfriend's number, but still no response. I didn't want to call his mother because she might sense something was wrong. So later that night, around nine o'clock, Danny girl finally answered the phone.

"They picked us up Billy," she said. The sadness in her voice was contagious.

"Are you and the baby alright?" I asked her.

"Yes, we're okay, but we are missing him already," she said.

There were tears rolling down her cheeks, I could tell by the sound of her voice. She said that she was allowed to talk to him for about 5 minutes. He said that they are going to be moving him. I immediately called Mr. Hawthorne, and he called the prosecutor.

"Are you willing to turn yourself in?" he asked me.

"If not, you got to let me know because I cannot lie to this man. We have an understanding, okay? You have to trust me."

"Do I need to come home?"

"Just wait for me to call you back tomorrow," he said.

"Billy," Mr. Hawthorne said the next day. "You have been indicted, you and Danny. Your bank accounts have been frozen. They have shut down all of your businesses and confiscated all of your equipment. They are also in the process of questioning everyone who worked for you. They also have Mr. Johnson in custody. They are charging him with money laundering as well as asking him a lot of questions about you all, but he should be getting out soon. They talked with Mr. Tanner also, your business attorney. They are flying Danny in tonight," he paused. "So, when are you coming back?"

"I'll be there tomorrow," I said.

I solemnly sat in my apartment in Miami staring out of the window at the ocean, thinking to myself, 'When will I see you again,' an old Baby Face song; but I'm sure he wasn't talking about the streets. Ashlee called from the store and she said that we could meet for lunch if I was up to it. I told her I would be there in an hour. In the meantime, I got back to my meditative gazing at the ocean. Amazingly, I lost track of time, because the phone rang and it was Ashlee telling me that I was supposed to have met her at the restaurant four hours ago!

"I'm sorry," I said, meaning it. "I fell asleep."

"It's alright. Are you going to get yourself something to eat?"

"Yes, mother," I said, jokingly.

As soon as I hung up with Ashlee, the phone rang. It was Mr. Hawthorne.

"Billy, the Feds have just went to your grandmother's house with a search warrant for a safe that is supposed to contain a large amount of cash. They've already confiscated Danny's house and they have his mother downtown questioning her even as we speak," he said.

"Does she have an attorney?" I asked.

"Yes, as soon as I heard, I sent someone down there for her."

"Thank you, Mr. Hawthorne."

"She has not made any statements and they have not charged her with anything."

"Mr. Hawthorne, I will be there first thing tomorrow, ready to turn myself in," I said, feeling a sadness that I was too macho to let show in my voice. I had never been to jail before.

I stopped at Ashlee's store and apologized for forgetting about our dinner appointment, and she forgave me with sweet kisses all over my face. I could not get myself to tell her what was going on. Ashlee was street, no doubt, but she had allowed me to see a part of her that I never knew existed. I realized that beneath the hard facade of her street persona was a soft, caring and gentle woman. I did not want to see her hurt.

As soon as I left Ashlee, I decided to stop at a jewelry store and pick up a beautiful ring for Ashlee. I wanted her to know what I was feeling and to express it with my heart, words and finances. So I bought her a diamond solitaire ring valued at $60,000. It was beautiful and on the inside it had an inscription that read, 'The World Is Ours.'

"Baby, I might be afraid to wear this without security," she said, smiling widely. "But with you I feel secure."

That night we went out to see a movie and dinner. I told her that I had to go back tomorrow.

"Well, which one of the house do you like?" she asked me, never really noticing my apprehensions about tomorrow. I think that was the hardest role I ever had to play in my life.

"I'll make a decision when I get back," I said. Ashlee was so happy.

At 9 o'clock the next morning, Ashlee dropped me off at the airport for my flight back to Nashville.

"Be careful baby and hurry back," she said, as I left her for my flight.

I knew I was not coming back. I went straight to Mr. Hawthorne's office as soon as I got back in town. It was evident that he was waiting on me, because his secretary hurried me to his office as if I were the President or something.

As I entered his office, he was on the phone. He pointed for me to have a seat. He stayed on the phone for about five more minutes before hanging up and looking at me seriously, saying, "That was our illustrious prosecutor. He wanted to know if you were going to volunteer your presence or should he send the Calvary after you. Don't worry, I told him you would be there," Mr. Hawthorne said, attempting to bring some humor to this unhumorous situation.

"Will I be able to get a bond?" I asked.

"I doubt it. He will vigorously oppose it. There is only one way that I could see him giving you a bond, and that is if you cooperate with him," he said straightforwardly.

"Billy, as your lawyer, I cannot tell you what to do, but I would advise you to not make any hasty decisions. Right now, you should leave all of your options open," he said. " And we'll cross those other bridges when we get to them. Billy, I have been working with these prosecutors for years and I can guarantee you, they'll lock their own mothers up if they feel confident that they can get the conviction." He paused for a minute.

"Billy, I hate to ask you this, but I must. Do you think that you can still afford my services? I can't take cash at this point either."

"Would you like your fee wired?" I asked, staring at him soberly in the eyes. He broke contact.

"Please understand Billy, this is business."

"Can I use your phone?" I asked, calming down considerably.

"I intend to pay for Danny and his mother's legal fees as well, so it will be one lump sum. Who shall I wire this money to?" "Make it out to the Law firm." I called Mr. Wolfe.

"Hello Mr. Wolfe, this is Mr. Ruth," I said.

"Hello, Mr. Ruth, can I get your confirmation code?" he asked. I gave him the code number we had worked out for transactions such as this one. I told him how much and where to transfer the money to.

"It'll be about an hour," I told Mr. Hawthorne, after hanging up the phone.

Mr. Hawthorne and I talked for an hour about how we would proceed from this point on. He asked me if I was satisfied with the direction he was going to be taking my case, if worse comes to worse. I said for right now I'm cool.

Maybe twenty minutes later, we headed over to the FBI building. Danny's lawyer was already there when we arrived. We walked to a glass-encased receptionist-like area. Mr. Hawthorne explained to her that I was turning myself in and in a very normal manner she proceeded to make a call. She acted as if this was the norm for her and I guess it was. Two agents came out and very politely cuffed me and took me through a door where I was fingerprinted and photoed. This all lasted about an hour, then I was taken to a holding cell, and to my surprise, Danny was already in there, laid back staring at the ceiling. What a hell of a reunion. His cell was directly across from mine, so we could see one another clearly.

"Danny, what's up?" I asked, feeling slightly comforted that my man was with me. Not that I wanted this, but if it had to be this way, at least we were together through this storm.

"Right now, I cannot call it man," he said. How's my mother?"

I told him that his mother was alright, which was true and I told him that I made sure that she had a lawyer.

At our bond hearing, we were both denied, because the prosecutor claimed that there was evidence that we posed a flight risk, as well as danger to society. My lawyer argued vehemently the fact that I turned myself in, but to no avail. The judge was not trying to hear it. After the bond hearing, we were transferred to a county jail. The same jail Mark, Dante and Mack were being held at until our arrest, then they were transferred outside of the county.

"That's what they do when you're working for the Government," one of my cell-mates said one day while we were discussing snitches and stuff.

When Ashlee found out about my arrest, she was on the first plane out of Florida headed in the direction of Nashville. I knew she would, but I just couldn't stand to tell her the truth and have to deal with the burden of her sadness, because in all truth I never wanted to hurt her, but I knew that this definitely would do that.

Mr. Hawthorne came to see me and he brought me a copy of the indictment. He told me, "These are the charges that the Government has brought against you." In a
nutshell, the charges were:

Count (1)

21 U.S.C 846 Conspiracy to distribute/possess with the intent to distribute cocaine

Count (2)

18 U.S.C 1956 (h) Money Laundering conspiracy to promote unlawful activity

Count (3)

21 U.S.C 841 (a) (1) Possession with intent to distribute

18 U.S.C. 2 Cocaine (aiding and abetting)

Count (4)

18 U.S.C. 924 (c) (1) Use/Carry of firearm in relation to drug trafficking

Count (5)

18 U.S.C. 4042 (b) Drug Trafficking

Chapter 14

"Billy, the Government has Mark, Dante and Mack on their side," Mr. Hawthorne was explaining to me about four months after me and Danny's arrest and indictment.

"They also have eight different statements from eight different people talking about what you all were doing," he paused for effect. "Now Billy, I know that you are not going to work for the Government, right?"

He asked as if my mind had ever been inclined to change.

"Of course not," I said, getting slightly irritated with the pleading sound of his voice.

"We've got to get ready for trial," he said.

I was worried about how things were going to turn out for Danny and I, but I was also secure in the knowledge that Ashlee and my child would be safe, because I was the only person in the click who actually knew who our true benefactor was. And I was not about to talk. Danny was still with me and he and I decided that going to trial was our only option. The Government wanted us to turn over all our assets and admit the part we played in the conspiracy, as well as who we were copping from. This is where the decision to go to trial became cemented into our minds. They said that if we cooperated with them, we'd get a nice deal.

"If you work with them, they are offering you a deal for 5 to 10 years, but if you play hardball and go to trial, you are facing at least 30 years," Mr. Hawthorne said, on the day we were picking a jury. "Billy, the D.A. says that he doesn't want you, he only wants the people you are dealing with, but if you're going to waste the people's money on this trial, he will seek the stiffest punishments he can. Which one would you choose?"

The Game Is Over!!!

Epilogue

95% of the people who catch a federal case will be in the same situation as Billy and Danny (What will they do?).

I wrote this story to tell everyone that the game is over! I sit here in this federal prison thinking was it all worth it. I don't think so, to be separated from my kids, family, to have your life put on hold. To be told what to eat, lights out at 11:30 during the week, and on weekends they go out at 2:30. This is not the life for anyone.

Now, let's get into what you are facing when you catch a federal case. First, you have **Federal Mandatory Minimum Sentencing Laws**. What are the mandatory minimum sentences? Mandatory minimum sentencing laws require harsh automatic prison terms for those convicted of certain crimes. Most often drug crimes. What sentences do federal drug offenders receive? A first time offender would receive a <u>Mandatory five year sentence</u> for:

- 1 gram of LSD
- 100 plants or 100 kilos of marijuana
- 5 grams of crack cocaine
- 500 grams of powder cocaine
- 100 grams of heroin
- 5 grams of methamphetamine
- 100 grams of PCP]

A first time offender would receive a <u>mandatory ten year sentence</u> for:

- 10 grams of LSD
- 1,000 plants or 1,000 kilos of marijuana
- 50 grams of crack cocaine
- 5 kilos of powder cocaine
- 1 kilo of heroin
- 50 grams of methamphetamine
- >>100 grams of PCP

You have to serve 85% of whatever time you receive. No parole, you get 54 days a year good time, and if you get into trouble while serving your time, they will take that away. The average time in the federal system is ten years (If you get ten years, they call that whining, 'no' time in here. People are glad to get that). You will have to serve eight and a half years of that ten years sentence. Now let's get in to how they give you your time.

In federal prosecutions, a defendant's sentence is largely determined by the United States sentencing guidelines (U.S.S.G.). Congress enacted the U.S.S.G. through the United Sentencing Commission. The Commission's responsibilities are to decrease the disparities in sentences among defendants. In order to achieve such objectives, the commission developed a sentencing grid, commonly known as the Sentencing Guidelines.

The guidelines became effective on November 1, 1987, and applies to federal offenders who committed their crimes after this date. At the hearing of the guidelines is a sentencing table which consists of a horizontal grid of six criminal history categories that intersects at each category with a vertical grid of forty-three offense level categories.

Sentencing Table

(In months of imprisonment)

Criminal History Category (Criminal History Points)

Level	Offense Gravity Score	Example Offenses	0	1	2	3	4	5	RFEL	REVOC	AGG/MIT
Level 4 Incar	13	Murder 3	60-120	66-120	72-120	78-120	84-120	90-120	96-120	120	+12/-12
	12	Drug delivery resulting in death; PWID cocaine, etc. (> 1000 gms)	54-72	57-75	60-78	66-84	72-90	78-96	84-102	120	+12/-12
	11	Rape; IDSI; robbery (I&B); agg assault (SBI); PWID cocaine, etc. > 100-1000 gms)	42-60	45-63	48-66	54-72	60-78	66-84	72-96	120	+12/-12
	10	Voluntary manslaughter; arson (person inside); PWID cocaine, etc. > 50-100 gms)	30-48	33-51	36-54	42-60	48-66	54-72	60-84	120	+12/-12
Level 3 Incar Cnty Jail/ RIP trade	9	Burglary (home, person pres.); agg. assault (cause S/W w/expns); robbery (threat SBI); robbery OHI; DUI agg assault (alt. SBI; agg. ind. asslt; PWID cocaine, etc. (>10-50 gms)	6-20	12-27	15-30	21-36	27-42	33-48	39-60	—	+6/-6
	8	Invol. mansl., homicide by veh. (when DUI); PWID cocaine, etc. (2.5-10 gms); PWID marijuana (>10-50 lbs.); arson (pers. not pres.); theft ($50,001-$100,000)	6-18	9-21	12-24	18-30	24-36	30-42	36-48	—	+6/-6
	7	Invol. mansl., homicide by vehicle (no DUI); statutory rape; theft ($25,001-$50,000)	4-12	7-15	10-18	16-24	22-30	28-36	34-42	—	+6/-6
	6	Agg assault (attempt SI w/weapon); burglary (not a home, person present); arson (property); escape (secure facility); PWID cocaine, etc. (<2.5 gms)	3-9	6-11½	9-15	12-18	15-21	18-24	21-27	—	+3/-3
Level 2 Incar RIP RS	5	Burglary (not a home, no one pres.); theft (> $2000-$25000); corruption of minors; firearms (loaded); robbery (remove property by force); PWID marijuana (1-10 lbs.)	RS-6	1-6	3-9	6-11½	9-15	12-18	15-21	—	+3/-3
	4	Indecent assault; forgery (w/$, etc.); firearms (unloaded); criminal trespass (breaks into buildings)	RS-3	RS-6	RS-9	3-9	6-11½	9-15	12-18	—	+3/-3
	3	Theft ($200-$2000); PWID marijuana (<1 lb); drug possession; forgery (money, etc.); REAP; simple assault; retail theft (3rd, subsequent)	RS-RIP	RS-3	RS-6	RS-9	3-9	6-11½	9-15	—	+3/-3
Level 1 RS	2	Theft ($50 - <$200); bad checks; retail theft (1st, 2nd > $150); retail theft (2nd < $150);	RS	RS	RS-RIP	RS-3	RS-6	1-6	3-9	—	+3/-3
	1	Most misdemeanor 3's; drug paraphernalia; small amount of marijuana; theft (< $50)	RS	RS	RS-RIP	RS-RIP	RS-3	RS-6	RS-6	—	+3/-3

(Source: Federal Sentencing Guidelines / www.ussc.gov)

To achieve a defendant's sentence for a particular offense, a court must determine the defendant's criminal history category and his corresponding base offense level for the instant offense. Once this is achieved, then the sentence is determined at the point where the two categories intersect within the sentencing table.

A defendant's criminal history is determined by calculating a certain amount of points, depending upon the particular past conviction being evaluated. In order to achieve a criminal history of one, two, three, four, five or six, a defendant's points must be 0-1, 2-3, 4-5, 79, 10-12 and 13 or more respectfully. Once a defendant's criminal history points reaches thirteen or above, he is placed in the highest possible criminal history category of six.

A defendant's past convictions determine the amount of points to be contributed toward his criminal history. For example, a defendant could receive one point for each driving violation or marijuana ticket, up to a total of six points. A defendant would also receive three points for each past conviction which accompany a term of imprisonment exceeding one year or more, whether or not the sentence was actually served. For example, if a defendant has two past convictions for driving while intoxicated, two past marijuana tickets, a past domestic violence which carried a two year sentence, and a past burglary where he served sixteen months in the county jail, the defendant would receive a point for each driving violation, a point for each marijuana ticket, three points for the domestic violence conviction, and three points for the past burglary conviction; for a total of ten criminal history points for a criminal history category of five.

However, if the defendant committed the federal offense less than a year from being released from an institution after serving a sentence upon a conviction, he would receive an additional two points or an additional one point if two points have already been added as a result of the defendant being on probation or parole. Therefore, three additional points to a defendant in the above example, would increase his total points to thirteen and place him in a criminal history category of six.

Furthermore, the Sentence Commission has developed a guideline manual with codes to aid in the determination of which past criminal conduct is to receive a particular amount of points, and in determining which base offense level should be accorded towards the instant offense.

The guideline manual provides predetermined offense levels depending upon the crime involved and its particular offense characteristics. For example, if a defendant has been found guilty for possession with the intent to distribute more than fifty grams of crack cocaine, but less than a hundred and fifty grams, he would receive a base offense level of thirty-two. Therefore, if one defendant had a criminal history category of five and another defendant with a criminal history of six, and each had a base offense level of thirty-two, they would receive a sentence between 188-235 and 210-262 months respectfully.

However, if the above defendants were convicted of distributing a hundred and fifty grams of crack cocaine, but less than five hundred grams, they would receive a base offense level of thirty-four with a sentencing range of 235-293 and 262-327 months respectfully.

In the federal justice system, crack cocaine is multiplied a hundred to one times greater than powder cocaine. Therefore, it requires that a defendant distribute five thousand grams of powder cocaine before he could receive the equivalent base offense level of thirtytwo, as that of a defendant who has distributed fifty grams of crack cocaine.

Crack cocaine is commonly prepared by adding five grams of powder cocaine and a gram of baking soda to quarter glass of extremely hot water. Once the powder cocaine has solidified into a gel, cold water is then added to produce a solid rock-like substance, which would equate to a weight of approximately four and a half grams of crack.

Drop the Gun or Face a Mean Federal Sentence

Furthermore, multiple offenses charged within the same indictment are calculated by using a conversion chart provided within the guideline manual. For example, if a defendant is indicted for distributing fifty grams of crack cocaine while possessing a hand gun, he would receive a base offense level of thirty-two for the crack and an additional four points for the hand gun, which would result in a total offense level of thirty-six.

Hearsay: Gossip. Statements Made by Someone Regarding a Third Party Based Solely on Someone's Belief or Assumption of the Truth.

In 1983, Congress passed into statute a law permitting hearsay evidence admissible in federal criminal prosecution. This means a person can be convicted in a federal trial solely on the testimony of another person without any physical evidence to corroborate such testimony. Furthermore, there are statutes in the federal system commonly known as "conspiracy statutes". Such hearsay testimony and conspiracy statutes has resulted in over 92% conviction rate in all federal drug prosecution.

CONSPIRACY: (1) An Unlawful Plot (2) A Conspiring Group

A conspiracy consists of an agreement between two or more individuals to commit an illegal act and an overt act toward achieving such objective of the crime. For example, defendant "A" is caught selling three kilograms of cocaine to an undercover agent. He then goes to the grand jury and testifies that defendants "B", "C", and "D" has bought and sold drugs with him in the past. The Government then presents the grand jury with casual evidence such as phone records and photos to establish a relationship between defendants "B", "C" and "D" with defendant "A" and drug trafficking.

Over 75% of all federal drug offenders are convicted under the conspiracy theory without ever being caught with any drugs. Solely upon the testimony of defendant "A", defendants "B", "C" and "D" can receive a conviction under the conspiracy statutes. In most cases, a defendant is wholly depended upon whether or not the jury believes defendant "A's" testimony or the Government's version of the facts.

Additionally, under the conspiracy theory a defendant can be accountable for all the acts and quantity of drugs sold or possessed by each co-defendant during the life of the conspiracy. In the above illustration, it is more probable that after the conspiracy has been established that defendants "A", "B" and "C" will plead guilty and testify against "D" in exchange for a sentence reduction.

Plead- (1) To Present a Plea in a Law Court (2) To Make an Appeal; Beg

In the federal system, there are three types of pleads a defendant can enter into with the Government:

1. The Government can make a recommendation to the court that a certain sentence is appropriate for the disposition of the case; however, such is not binding upon the court and if the court rejects such recommendation, the defendant will not be permitted to withdraw his plea.

2. The Government agrees not to oppose a particular sentence the defendant may request of the court; however, the court is not bounded and the defendant will not be permitted to withdraw the plea in the event that the court rejects such proposal.

3. The Government and defendant agree that a particular sentence is appropriate for the disposition of the case; however, the court is not bounded, but if it rejects such agreement, the defendant will be permitted the opportunity to withdraw his plea.

Furthermore, in the federal system, the court is bound by mandatory minimum sentence for particular crimes in the absence of special circumstances. Therefore, a court is not permitted to go below a certain sentence, unless there is a provision within the guideline manual that authorizes the court to depart downward.

Again, a defendant's sentence in a drug conspiracy is determined by the drug quantity contributed to him in the overall conspiracy and any particular offense characteristics.

In determining the appropriate sentence, a judge may consider a variety of conduct within the conspiracy to increase a defendant's offense level points. For example, if defendant "A" assaults a person during the conspiracy, defendant "B" can receive additional points to his offense level if the court determines that defendant "B" was reasonably foreseeable of the conduct of defendant "A". Furthermore, if a defendant is convicted of conspiracy to distribute two thousand grams of powder cocaine, there is no guarantee that will be the only amount accountable to him in establishing his base offense level. For example, if defendant "A" gives a statement that defendant "B" gave him a thousand grams of the two thousand in which he later convert into crack; defendant "B" offense level would be established by the thousand grams he retained and an additional hundred thousand grams for the thousand which defendant "A" converted into crack for a total drug amount of a hundred and one thousand grams of cocaine.

> *An Investigative Report Conducted by the Probation Office used to Compile an Accurate History of the Defendant (Accused).*
>
> *Completed Prior to Sentencing, It Includes Prior Arrests, Drugs and/or Alcohol Use, Family History etc.*

When the defendant is either found guilty or pleads guilty, the court will defer sentencing for approximately three months to refer the defendant to a probation officer who will prepare a presentence report (PSI). The PSI is crucial to the federal sentencing scheme. It is the primary source from which the court relies upon in its determination of the appropriate sentence for a particular defendant.

Primarily, there are two options available to a defendant in order to receive a time deduction from an otherwise appropriate sentencing range. Normally, a defendant would receive either a two or three point deduction from his base offense level depending upon how early he accepted responsibility for his conduct within the offense. However, if the defendant contests any of the essential facts within the conduct of the conspiracy, the probation officer can determine that the defendant has not accepted responsibility and recommend that the court deny any reduction based upon such determination.

Substantial Assistance- Tell Everything You Know

The other option available to a defendant is to provide substantial assistance to the Government in the prosecution of other individuals. Pursuant to 5K1, in the U.S. guideline manual, the prosecutor may submit a motion to the court that a certain amount of points be deducted from a defendant's offense level. Normally, the amount of such deduction will largely depend upon how substantial the assistance that the defendant provides is to the Government.

There is a variety of options available to the defendant in order to obtain such deductions. He can testify at the grand jury to bring about the indictment of other individuals. He can testify at the trial of other individuals on behalf of the Government. Furthermore, he can work with the Government in establishing other conspiracies through control sells or purchase of drugs.

In federal prosecutions, there is no consequences if you sell drugs to a Government agent or informant or you purchase drugs from them. Traditionally, a defendant will give information and testimony against those individuals he has sold drugs to, instead of those he has purchased drugs from. This is largely due to the fact that he will usually have more individuals he has sold drugs to; thus, more individuals to offer to the Government for a greater sentence reduction. For example, while working with the Government, defendant "A" offers to sell defendant "B" two kilograms of cocaine for $25,000 (a very substantial deduction from the average cost). However, the conspiracy is established if defendant "B" agrees. Additionally, if defendant "B" takes any steps toward trying to secure a deal, that an overt act is established and a great probability exists that defendant "B" will be convicted.

A defendant will not receive a reduction for substantial assistance until he has performed the above function for the Government.

Pursuant to Federal Rules of Criminal Procedure 355, a defendant can offer the Government substantial assistance any time during the period if completing three years on a nine year sentence when he read in his city's newspaper that defendant "B", who he has had a drug dealing relationship with in the past, has recently been indicted on drug charges. Defendant "A" could immediately contact the U.S. Attorney and offer to testify against defendant "B" in exchange for a time reduction.

In preparing the PSI, the probation officer will interview each defendant in the conspiracy, other witnesses and the U.S. Attorney while evaluating the offense characteristics in making the appropriate determination of each defendant's offense level and criminal history points.

Immediately after the PSI is prepared, the defendant and the prosecutor will be given the opportunity to offer any objections to the report. Immediately prior to the sentencing, the court will state orally on the record why it opposes one party's objections to the report over the other party.

Again, one defendant's offense characteristics and drug quantities can be contributed to other participants within the conspiracy for sentencing purposes. The court utilizes a "preponderance of the evidence" standard, as opposed to the "beyond a reasonable doubt" standard utilized by a jury in returning a verdict of guilt. Essentially, the burden of proof is less stringent than standard utilized at trial.

In most cases, the U.S. Attorney simply offers testimony of offense characteristics not charged in the indictment such as weapon possession and additional drug quantities. Again, any facts that a defendant disputes can be a determining factor of whether or not he will receive the three point deduction from his offense level for acceptance of responsibility. Furthermore, it is not until PSI is fully prepared that a defendant can reasonably ascertain what sentence maybe imposed at the sentence hearing. In 72% of cases, the court will accept the PSI version as it is submitted by the probation officer.

The admission of hearsay into evidence and the lack of proof needed to establish a conspiracy, has produced the common scenario of defendant's exaggerating and fabricating evidence and testimony in order to escape the harsh punishment of the federal sentencing scheme by offering another individual in place of themselves. It has become a familiar occurrence in the federal system where brothers have offered up brothers, sons have offered up mothers and fathers have offered up daughters. It appears that no one is exempted from the snare of the conspiracy law. A young black woman named Kendra Smith served approximately nine years on a twenty-two year sentence for simply having a boyfriend who sold drugs, before President Clinton granted her a pardon prior to leaving office. An Arkansas mother received a three year sentence for receiving seven hundred dollars from her son's childhood friend, who claimed it was payment toward a loan owed to her son. An Illinois college sophomore received a five year sentence for simply receiving money toward his school expenses from his uncles, who were dealing drugs.

The drug trade has become an alluring, seemingly irresistible temptation for urban minorities in the face of North America and Asia Free Trade Agreement, which has depleted an already highly competitive middle class job market, which would otherwise be available. Additionally, the high illiteracy rate, social poverty and dysfunctional family structure among such groups has made the drug trade an enticing option to escape the psychological and social inferiority complex perpetuated through corporate America; and to offer such individuals an otherwise unavailable opportunity into the world of entrepreneurship; thus, into the illusionary world of selfpride and independence.

However, not only is the drug trade reaping havoc upon our communities, but it is destroying the lives and families of those who unfortunately find themselves in the inescapable snare of the federal conspiracy net.

We must resist! The choice is yours.

Notes

Kevin Robinson

Email: krobpublishing615@gmail.com

629-266-1124

Made in the USA
Columbia, SC
10 March 2023

13529532R00052